AF432419

Praise for *Stalking Unicorns*

"Coveny has given us an emotional roller-coaster as she charts her family's move to California and subsequent return to the East Coast. We get a keen sense of a close-knit family, but also a marvelous depiction of mores in Silicon Valley. Coveny is that rare thing—a wry writer with a great heart. You can read her for the shrewdness and you can read her for the distilled feeling. In truth, you will read her for both."
Baron Wormser, author of *Songs of a Voice* and *The Road Washes Out in Spring*

"Frenetic, edgy, satirical, it's Mad Men meets Hunter S. Thompson. The narrator's rapier wit skewers the world of Silicon Valley, in prose that is faster than 5 gig. We see a host of colorful West Coast characters as the husband Gordo hopes to get in on "an unprecedented trajectory," only to find out that "Silicon Valley culture was filled with Mad Hatters and Queens of Hearts disguised as tech moguls and neighbors." Narrated with humor and insight, it is the keen eye and satiric wit of the writer, as well as her unfailing devotion to family that drives the heart of this story."

–Michael C. White, author of *Soul Catcher* and *Beautiful Assassin*

"A heart-breaking, honest and riveting story that underscores the power of staying open, fighting for what you believe, loving with your whole heart and never giving up on each other. It is a tribute to own capacity for growth and redemption. Once you begin this adventure, you will not be able to put it down."
–Kristin Peck, author of *Perseverance*, podcaster of *On Purpose* and Fortune 500 CEO

STALKING UNICORNS

Kelly Coveny

STALKING UNICORNS

Draft2Digital

PO box 2860

Broken Arrow, OK 74013

Library of Congress Cataloging-in-Publication Data

Names: Coveny, Kelly, author

Title: Stalking Unicorns/Kelly Coveny

ISBN 979-8-224-97021-6

This memoir is a personal account of the author's experiences and recollections. Names, characters, businesses, places, events, and incidents are either the products of memory or used in a fictitious manner. Any resemblance to actual persons, living or dead, or actual events is purely coincidental. While every effort has been made to respect privacy and maintain the accuracy of events and narratives, certain liberties may have been taken in storytelling for narrative cohesion or privacy concerns.There are embellishments and this not necessarily an accurate accounting or narrative of things that have happened, but rather the story is told in a way, using certain creative liberties, to convey some subjective experience of the author.

The views and opinions expressed in this memoir are solely those of the author and do not reflect the views of any individual, organization, or entity that the author may or may not have been associated with in a professional or personal capacity, unless explicitly stated.

BOOK DESIGN by milk* *www.milksono.com*

Acknowledgements

There was the life experience and the book experience. I am graced to have people who guided me through both. Joe– my constant, caring, championing reader of all umpteen versions. Your compassion and encouragement carried me. Leo and Finn– for lovingly listening to chapters and inspiring resilience. You are my wild blue yonder and my home sweet home. Ashley– for seeing the inner unicorn and holding me accountable. Your literary discernment, deep humanity and gentle guidance made this book what it is. Bill and Baron–for believing in my imagination and teaching me to pay attention. Nathalie– your cultural insights, life-saving humor, and devil-may-care daring was fuel.

I am deeply grateful to our friends in California. Lisa and Danny– for their unwavering kindness and boundless support. Few people in life 'show up' the way you did. Dante had Virgil, we had you. Julie and Jeff– for being islands of joy in a stormy sea. Hsinya– for welcoming us and enabling us to leave with grace and compassion. Samantha– for being the catalyst that set it in motion. Jim– for saving us from false incrimination, bankruptcy, and jail. Prerna– for legal counsel that opened my heart and mind.

To my family and friends back home– Kristin and Bob– our lighthouse in a turbulent sea. Your steadfast love helped us see beyond where we were. Amy– my fellow pioneering adventurer. Your fierce love and unstoppable courage inspired and buoyed me. Marlon– for accompanying me through invisible jungles and making me laugh. Our dear Westport friends– for sending us off with joy, welcoming us back with love and supporting us along the way.

Table of Contents

Preface

Part One: California Dreaming

Stuck in Stucco Prison with a Fake Ficus

The Shyster Shaman Shake-Down Tour

Betting the Farm on a Wrap-Around Ranch

A Red-Bearded Narcissist Delivers the Dream

Burnout and Bloody Mary's in Half Moon Bay

Navigating Bi-Coastal Breakdowns with a Bucket Hat

Part Two: Welcome to Wonderland

Greeted by Shrieking Goats and a Gadfly

Pitching Paradise with Fat Black Crows

If Only the Assassins Guild Served Cookies

Sampling Plumcots with Hairy-Toed Men

Entering a Sri Lankan Temple and Pigeon Pose

Capping Off Chaos with Nuclear Orange Parasites

Part Three: Escape from Hell

Towering Inferno of Beef and Tijuana Black Box

Fire-eating Goblins and a Sky Full of Drones

Choosing Electric Bikes over Adult Diapers

Child Services, Shotguns, and a Jumbo Popcorn

Confronting the King of Spam and a Red-Headed Troll

Hunting for Houses and a White-Collar Criminal

Serving Pomegranate Martinis and Pancakes

Part Four: Surviving a Tsunami

Torching the Job Before the Big Getaway

Dumping Dog Beds at Midnight in Laguna Beach

Profanity, Stinkbugs and Personal Metamorphosis

Recruiting a German Nanny for Crisis Control

Saved by a School Algorithm and Men in Blue

Entertaining Jail Threats and a Good Sunrise

Kiss Dolls, Star Wars, and Exit Strategies

Part Five: Going Home

Calculating the Cost of Sacrifice

Twisted Truths and Magic Shrooms

Getting Past Penis Envy and Alligators

Navigating Brain Fog and Ego Death

Plotting a Pipedream and Saying Goodbye

Unravelling Old Stories and Tying Up Loose Ends

Dreams fuel the spirit.

"Can we pet him," I asked. Lightning was a blind, deaf Sicilian donkey with a dark mane that formed a cross along his shoulders and back. He was eating grass in the back pasture. I was seven months pregnant and ready for adventure.

"He will kill you with one kick," our landlord said flatly. *Not me,* I thought, *I will ride Lightning off into a fiery blaze of glory.*

Passion does not abide by parameters.

Two teenage sons later we set out on an urgent pilgrimage to chase down our dream. These stories chronicle the adventures that ensued over a two-year, bi-coastal blitz from Connecticut's gold-coast to Silicon Valley and back. We'd wow them with wit, grit, and marketing savvy. No idea our New England wonder was for wannabees. Billion-dollar ideas were the new bar.

Transactional was the new transformational.

No one dabbles in adrenalin. The addiction to coming attractions is real. The gateway drug to success is hope and start-up culture's the ultimate dope. Work harder, longer, faster– score. Dream bigger, bolder– imagine more. Empty promises were everywhere. Angel A … Series B. Tomorrow seduces. No way to see. We could not have forecast what followed.

Catastrophe is a catalyst.

Plan B was less pie-in-the-sky; more 007 meets *Survivor*. Escape cannabis Alcatraz without going bankrupt or being incriminated in white collar crime. It escalated from there. Suicide threat, dog attack trial, abusive renters. Hypervigilance invaded every corner of my life. Hopelessness prevailed. Therapy failed. I needed unorthodox help. Not more thinking about my thinking.

Curiosity is the antidote to despair.

My mind was under siege. So, when a friend suggested I micro-dose psilocybin mushrooms, I was all in. How bad could a mushroom be? Psilocybin *was* a narcotic, but micro-dosing was headed mainstream. Transforming the future of mental health. Why stop at me? Why not start an underground empire? My imagination ran wild. Adventure feeds the soul.

Why ride Lightning when you could stalk unicorns?

Part One:

California Dreaming

Stuck in Stucco Prison with a Fake Ficus

Late-stage Silicon Valley cannabis goldmine– *that's* the wave we were going to ride. Pioneer the last great branding frontier. It required moving two teenage boys, two golden retrievers, a house and life across the country. But it was the adventure of a lifetime. My husband, Gordo, would be Chief Branding Officer for Canna Bliss, the largest cannabis company in North America. Odysseys come with sacrifices.

The big Canna Bliss Executive Retreat fell on the weekend of my 50th birthday blow-out bash. So, we cancelled it. I didn't really care. Paying top dollar for a boatload of people to power-eat sushi and guzzle Grey Goose seemed gratuitous anyway. I was disappointed but I'd celebrate with the people who mattered. Plus, the bigger picture seemed worth it… right up until I googled the location. *The Black Forest Lodge*. It looked appalling. Trophy animal heads. Cafeteria-style, fat-food. It advertised *rustic authenticity.*

Sunday morning, my husband Gordo and I were drinking coffee in the sunroom. "Was Big Sur booked?" I asked, "Because in a state of Pebble Beach options, surely they could have done better than The Black Forest Lodge." Rain pelted the skylights.

He didn't look up from texting, *"Less distractions,"* he said.

"Sounds like code for *cheapskate CEO*," I replied. And aren't *lodges* more of a Montana thing," I reached in front of him and broke off a dead orchid bloom.

"Start-ups act differently," he replied.

"Sounds suspect," I said.

"We're going to have to roll with it," he responded. I rolled my eyes.

Rolling with it was not one of my core attributes. In my early 20's I tele-marketed truck parts and wrote WWF promo copy for a skinny ad guy with a pencil tie who promised 'upward mobility in marketing'. After two months of walking through the urine-scented vestibule, I quit. All future positions were subject to the 'lobby test'. No marble, no go. Full-stop at fake Ficus trees. Empty promises always have tell-tale signs.

But late-stage start-up*s* are impossible to read. Just a big invisible *Enter at Your Own Risk* sign as you open the door. *Less distractions* was either a brilliant tactic or bogus propaganda. The future could be a raucous rally cry filled with epic anticipation and greatness to come. Or it could be a nonstop, late-night, yell-fest over gelatinous pizza with foul-mouthed metro-sexual boy-men on the verge of losing funding. Two weeks later Gordo left for The Black Forest Lodge.

"I'm calling you from a giant redwood near the parking lot," Gordo said. "It's the only spot with reception. We have a five-minute break. How are you?" he asked.

I was in a long line at CVS. "Forget *me*, how are *you*? How's it going?" I replied.

"Kels, the team is seriously the most talented group of executives I've ever worked with," he said. Gordo sees the good in everyone and everything. Me, less so. Overstatement is bound to disappoint.

"Not including your job with Richard Branson," I caveated quietly, trying not to be *that* person in line.

"It's kind of an all-star team," he said not dissuaded, "Ex-head of Nike runs retail. R&D guy did formulations for Burt's Bees. Beverage guy launched Zola. IT is from Google. M&A from Goldman. It's kind of crazy," he said. It did sound impressive, but we still didn't have a formal offer.

"Did you talk to Dirk," I asked.

"Briefly," Gordo replied, "He asked if I was on board. I said yes, depending on the offer and my wife meeting him."

I clenched my fist. "*What?*" I said, "Why did you say *that*? He's going to think you're weak."

Gordo was emphatic, "I could care less. It matters to me what you think. He *was* a little surprised. Don't think he's heard that a lot. But I told him I'm moving my whole family across the country. Obviously, it matters what my wife thinks." I loved that Gordo always put our family first. "One more day of presentations. Home day after tomorrow. I love you Kels," he said.

"Love you too," I replied.

Gordo returned a man on fire. I heard the car service pull down our gravel driveway and ran out to meet him. He swung his backpack over his shoulder and gathered me into his arms. His smile was wild with conviction. I hadn't seen that look since we first met, and he was running billions in business for IPG.

"Sky's the limit," he said.

We marched into the house. Planted ourselves on the couch.

"Tell me everything," I replied excited.

Gordo was sitting but his energy was electric. "I presented my vision for branding the second night. The executive team gave me a standing ovation. Afterward, Dirk texted me to meet him in the bar. He wrote a number on a napkin and slid it over. I told him I'd need double that if he wanted me. He said *not going to happen.* I stood up, smiled, thanked him, and said I'd have to take a pass. An hour later, between salary, stock options and bonus, we got to my number."

Gordo's confidence was contagious. I smiled and hugged him. "That is AMAZING," I said. "Obviously, he's putting all that in writing?" I asked.

"Yup," Gordo replied, "Plus, he promised whatever budget I need. The autonomy to run marketing, move the office, hire you as the creative director AND launch *Evolve the Conversation* as our event program."

I felt like a little kid at Christmas. "Really? He was on board with the idea of luminaries exploring a single word? He didn't find it too lofty or hard to monetize?" I asked. I'd been pitching the idea for two years. Packaged it to Hyatt as *Travel the World. To* Grey Goose as *The Spirit of Conversation.* Everyone loved it. No one could figure out how it made money.

"Dirk said event programs are my call," Gordo said, "Kels, *ETC* is finally going to get the platform it deserves."

I was excited but promises can be broken. "Wow, that would be incredible. Is he putting that in writing too?" I asked.

"They just raised $850 million. It's not going to be an issue. We *are* going to have to take a leap of faith with some of this stuff."

My throat tightened. Leaping has its pitfalls. Plotting and planning was one thing. The reality of moving across the country was quite another. We'd have to leave our beautiful home for the big unknown. Our boys had great friends. There, they'd be starting over. Luke was headed for D1 lacrosse. Out there, it was barely a sport. Finley had a top-notch IEP resource team. There, we'd be rolling the dice. Leaving paradise to pioneer a dream. The obvious option was for Gordo to commute until we knew if the job delivered. But we are a close family unit. The idea of separating filled me with dread. I made a pro/con list. Talked to my sisters, friends– even my parents' spirits. The response was unanimous. He should go. We should wait to follow.

Sensible choices rarely account for emotional context.

I knew Gordo wouldn't be his all-in self without us. He could do the job, but his heart would be divided. He'd be exhausted from the bi-monthly commute. I'd be overwhelmed by navigating the details of our daily life without him. Gordo is the ballast that keeps our ship afloat. Plus, we'd both spent time working in southern California. The three-hour time difference seems nominal, but it takes a toll. It would never work to split up. We'd need to stay together. The question was– should we go? Comfort cannot be underrated. But desire is a fire that must be fed. The reasons couldn't be mapped out.

Dreams never can.

A couple weeks later we flew to California for dinner with Dirk and his wife. Gordo would show me the corporate offices of Canna Bliss. We'd look for a rental and wrap up the trip with an afternoon getaway in Half Moon Bay. The office was in San Jose. I googled it. The downtown looked vibrant, charming– viable. We'd go somewhere fun for lunch. Expense it. Make up for my cancelled birthday bash. We exited the airport, got our rental car, and set off. I smiled with anticipation, the city skyline ahead. We weren't driving toward it.

"Gordo are you going the right way?" I asked, "The city is over there," I pointed north.

"The offices are *just on the outskirts*," he said. Rough translation: *I will hate them*. My heart sank. We pulled into the empty parking lot. "Must be a lot of people on sales calls today," Gordo added. My stomach turned. The Canna Bliss Corporate Office was a one-story stucco complex with no visible windows. My eyes filled up. Enthusiasm drained from every limb in my body. "Start-ups are a different animal," he explained. "I know how it looks. I had the same reaction but remember part of my package is setting up a marketing office anywhere we want. It will NOT be here. I promise you".

I took a deep breath. Okay. This was nothing more than a launchpad. I pulled myself together. We entered with East Coast flare. Heads high. Shoulders back. Wall Street swagger meets SoHo chic. Given the exterior, my lobby expectations were low. Not low enough. My eyes fell first on the fake Ficus with dusty leaves– probably plucked last-minute from the misfit clearance items at Home Goods. It hung sadly off-center on the tired beige wall below the stained drop-ceiling tiles. Straight ahead sat Myrtle. Gordo had told me about her, but she had to be experienced. Straight out of central casting for a relaunch of *Twin Peaks*, Myrtle had a dead-eye stare. Her face had settled into a Sanskrit etching that warned of danger. I fully expected her to appear from behind the Formica desk limping with a broom cane.

She greeted us without breaking a smile. "You must be Kelly," she said. "I'm Myrtle, you can sit in the visitor area while you wait for Gordo." I looked at Gordo with a flat expressionless triple exclamation.

There's a whole underground language couples use to communicate crucial information non-verbally. Rough synopsis: *Leave me anywhere at all in this godforsaken facility and I will be forced to craft weapons from office equipment and stage a full-blown coup.* Gordo's well-being frequently relies on his masterful reading of these messages. Myrtle escorted us to a cubicle quad where she was likely depositing me for an untold number of hours without food or drink.

"Coffee is in the community room," she said pointing to a kitchen hallway." I nodded. I trusted Gordo would shut it down. I forgot our marital spark is often fueled by twisted humor.

"She does some of her best thinking in cubicles, so this is perfect. Thank you," and then turning to me, "I shouldn't be more than a couple hours." I smiled. Game on.

"Of course, honey. Who should I call to order my triple-shot, no foam, caramel macchiato, and egg-white omelet?" Myrtle stared at me– her first impression confirmed. I was a high-maintenance, East-Coast WASP. Truth is, I take my coffee black and would never trust Myrtle to know where to get a proper egg-white omelet.

"You know what," Gordo said, "I'm going to show Kelly around." He grabbed my hand.

I turned back to Myrtle. I didn't want to make her feel bad or leave the wrong impression. She had a likely thankless job in an office that would make me want to stab my eyes out. "It's a pleasure to meet you and I love your dress. Such a fun print." It had a leopard pattern with bright green piping suggesting that outside of this miserable place she might be fun.

Her face lit up. "I thought so too. My twin sister and I got it at T.J. Maxx," she said.

"Let's go, don't want to keep anyone waiting," Gordo said.

"Great to meet you," I said to Myrtle, and we scurried off. Gordo showed me around. Introduced me to a handful of people. The vibe was more rural Pennsylvania than Silicon Valley. It had a hauntingly cockroach resiliency about it– like a dystopian series where sunlight is extinguished in chapter one, but everyone works on in darkness blinded by hope or greed or fear. Or all three.

The Shyster Shaman Shake-Down Tour

"Shiva is going to take you on a tour of the dispensary and grow facility if you want to go. It's kind of cool to see the process from seed to plant to sale." Gordo said. I'd never seen any of it.

"Sure. You'll meet me after?" I asked.

"Yes. She's going to pick you up out front." I walked back through the illustrious lobby and waited outside. Shiva pulled up and emerged from her Mercedes S Class wearing dream catcher earrings and a purple sweater with embroidered type that read: *Less egos. More amigos.* She had a faux-hippie, trust-fund baby, woo-woo vibe but I reserved a slim margin of latitude in case my read was wrong. "We are driving?" I asked.

"Yes," she replied, "It's a few miles away." She shook my hand. Held it too long. "You have a very strong life force," she said. "I hope that doesn't make you uncomfortable," she added.

"Not at all," I said getting into the car. "You should see it on a spin bike." I closed my door. The sales pitch was coming. There was no tone I could have used, no witty comeback I could have crafted to stop it. Normal handshakes have an expiration date. Not hers. My life force was *my* business. Not a dispensary tour conversation-starter. She clicked her seatbelt, and we pulled out of the parking lot.

"I understand you are moving here from the east coast. Must be stressful carrying the weight of the whole family," she said.

"Not at all," I lied, "Gordo is doing everything. My job in New York keeps me busy. Enough about me, I understand you play a pivotal role here," I said.

"My title is Plant Shaman. I am responsible for harnessing the positive power of plants and people," she said.

"That is quite a job," I responded.

"Well, start-ups can spin in crazy directions. So, it's important to keep the energy grounded and aligned." I nodded trying to imagine who approves such a role. "It keeps me up at night," she continued, "but I believe strongly in our mission." We pulled into a parking space. "In fact," she added, "I told Dirk I couldn't take a salary until spirit tells me it's time." Now it made sense. Unpaid role. Good PR spin. Zero risk. I exited the car.

"Great ride," I said attempting to shift topics.

She gently placed her hand on the hood. "A dear client left it to me after passing," she replied. There was no way I could take more than half an hour of this.

"How long is the tour," I asked.

"Two hours," Shiva said. I rolled my head back. "Are you okay," she asked. I nodded tersely, pulled open the heavy door, and held it for her. I probably shouldn't alienate everyone on the first visit. She stopped to make sincere eye contact, "We *could* do it in one and a half, but you'd miss the maternity ward where we bring the mother plants back to full strength."

Still holding the door, I gestured politely for her to walk through. "Sounds *wonderful*," I responded following behind her. "I *would* hate to miss that. Unfortunately, I have a work call in an hour. Gordo didn't tell me how long it would be. My apologies." The door guy scanned my license and gave me a badge.

Once through, she placed her hand on my shoulder, "Work can be so demanding," she said, "It blocks our ability to feel joy."

I made myself not flinch. Every ounce of me wanted to twist her hand behind her back and tell her to never touch me again. Had our son Luke been there, I would have bet him two hundred dollars, she'd take this opportunity to offer some form of service.

"I used to provide energy clearings. I retired a few years ago but I'd be happy to make an exception," she said.

"What a kind offer. I will keep that in mind," I replied walking immediately over to the Bud Bar. Muscular, tattooed Bud Tenders stood behind it ready to help. Glass cases were lined with all different marijuana strains as well as smoking, dosing, and drinking paraphernalia. The bar was set up like a deli counter. Hand-written signs featured *Daily Specials.* Beautifully crafted edibles displayed in a lower case. Canna Bliss had a sexy side. Epic relief.

I donned a full paper body suit, hair net, and footies before we entered the indoor grow. She *was* quite knowledgeable about the process but the masculine/ feminine energy banter over baby plants in the incubation room was a bit much. Vacuum-sealed double doors separated each section.

"The last room is where we prepare the dried plants for sale." Heavily tattooed black and Latino men used tweezers to extract buds from stems. "Beautiful job. Bless you Maurice," she said resting her hand on his shoulder. He smiled. Surely Maurice must want to weaponize those tweezers. I certainly did. But against all odds, his gratitude seemed sincere. We left the grow area. "Canna Bliss provides job opportunities for minorities wrongfully convicted on marijuana charges," she said.

We finished the tour in a windowless breakroom. Shiva stopped and closed her eyes. "You can feel the energy, right," she said.

I felt hungry and irritable. "Definitely," I replied, praying we were near the end.

She pointed to a small stone protruding from the concrete corner. "*That,*" she said, "is our north star. I brought it from Es Vedra in Ibiza– one of the most powerful magnetic fields in the world. It aligns our corporate chakras and grounds our future success." We stood in silence. She had to be sleeping with someone. Or more likely had info on someone who had. Or was the wife of some investor. We exited.

I gave her my paper suit. Gordo approached us. "I am also a life coach," Shiva said, "So, if you want support once you get here, I'd be happy to help. And since you are now part of the Canna Bliss family, the first session is my gift." Gordo greeted us. "Your wife is an old soul. Powerful energy," Shiva said, placing her hand on my forehead. I must have looked traumatized because Gordo grabbed her right shoulder emphatically, "

"YOU," he said pausing a few uncomfortable seconds, "are a gift, Shiva." He let the silence hang before letting go of her shoulder. Then more light-heartedly he added, "Thank you. We've got to run," and whisked me away.

Gordo's ancestors are from Sicily. He has an uncanny ability to frontload average language with a clear undertone of: *You are safe if you don't cross the line.*

"Where exactly does she fit into this puzzle?" I asked as we walked to the car.

"Plant Shaman," Gordo said. We were silent. "And daughter of the lead investor," he added.

I nodded, "That makes more sense." We waked to the car.

"Do you want to get lunch in San Jose?" he asked.

"Definitely not. Let's go to Palo Alto," I replied, "I found a place that's supposed to have great tacos."

Betting the Farm on a Wrap-Around Ranch

I might have loved San Jose. Might have left humming *Do You Know the Way…* but now it was dead to me forever. Mired in mediocrity. We got in the car. "Well, that was enlightening," I said as we pulled onto the 101.

"I'm not going to lie Kels, I had that uh-oh feeling the first time I came, but I figured people start businesses out of their garage. Success doesn't always come from the most likely places."

I leaned my head against the window. "Well, if our success is exponentially based off the inverse of their design skills, we will be billionaires," I said. We cruised down the 8-lane highway passing exits I'd never heard of. Would I one day meet up with girlfriends in *Los Altos* for margaritas? See a Marvel movie in *Mountainview*?

"We can turn around and go home today you know. Forget this whole thing. Chalk it up to a crazy adventure. Luke would be thrilled," Gordo said.

"I don't think it's fair to evaluate the whole company based off Myrtle, Shiva, and the fake Ficus. What do *you* think?" I asked.

Gordo paused before speaking, "I think it has all the right players. Investors are throwing cash at it. The board of directors is stacked with heavy hitters. But we're in this together and you usually have spot-on intuition, so if you think it's a mistake, we won't do it."

We pulled off at Embarcadero. I looked at my GPS. "It's called Gott's Roadside– on the corner of El Camino Real in the Town & Country mall. Like 2 ½ miles down on the right." I wasn't sure what I thought. The decision was too big to base on instinct alone. But facts were futile too. I wanted this to be our big break. I could see the boys in UC colleges, could picture Gordo and I eventually moving down to Malibu walking our dogs on the beach. I liked the weather. Liked the healthy lifestyle. Wanted to explore a new direction. I'd lost both my parents not too long ago. Lost my sense of peace after Finley was attacked by his friend's dog. I'd even lost interest in the confines of my career. We couldn't outrun any of it. I knew that. I just wanted to infuse some excitement back into our life. Feel the magic of momentum. Becoming pioneers in a growth industry headed for the moon seemed like a good strategy.

But Canna Bliss felt more like a carnival ride than a rocket ship. More glorified swamp than waterfront property. "I don't know," I finally responded, "Let's see how dinner with your boss goes." I pointed to the Gotts sign. Gordo pulled in and we got out. Classical music filled pergola-covered pathways. Terracotta-tiled roofs connected charming boutiques. No big box stores. Even the cafeteria-style ordering at Gott's had flare.

"I am starving," Gordo said as we sat down at the outdoor tables.

"Me too," I replied. We soaked in the sunshine, devoured our food, and digested the day. "Well," I said, "Palo Alto beats the hell out of San Jose."

Gordo stacked our trays to return. "Maybe we move the new office here," he said.

"Maybe," I replied, "Let's check out the shops,". We entered Blue Mercury.

An exuberant gay gentleman greeted us, "How can I help you?" he asked.

"Do you have anything that can remove stress, wrinkles and an uncertain future," I asked smiling.

"YES, I do," he said and with a flamboyant wave of his hand led me to the far wall. "Bee venom! It will erase the stress, plump up the future and…" He looked back at me. "I don't see any wrinkles, but it will help with those too." I bought it all. Hope springs eternal. Perhaps I'd go home looking twenty years younger. We perused the bookstore and a few jaunty clothing boutiques before getting hand-made ice cream at Tin Pot Creamery.

Palo Alto had risen to the top for best schools. Budget, dogs, and virtual tours had whittled our options down to two houses. We had showings the next day, but I'd become obsessed with a waterfront townhouse in Tiburon. "You ready to go to Marin," Gordo asked.

"I'm hoping it's not as far away as it looks. Thank you for being open to checking it out," I replied.

"You've been stalking it on realtor.com for weeks. I wouldn't miss it," Gordo said teasingly. We got in the car and headed out. Two hours later, we sat in gridlock traffic on the Golden Gate bridge.

"Okay, so, the commute is *not ideal*," I admitted, "But maybe you move the offices to Sausalito," I proposed.

We drove halfway to my dreamhouse before realizing Tiburon was in Siberia. On the way back we stopped in Mill Valley and wandered around. "It's charming– but a little dated, right," Gordo said. I looked at the low-slung roofs, earth tone exteriors.

"The architecture has a kind of 1970's hangover vibe," I replied. I looked at the women passing by. The dress was laid-back casual, yet art directed within an inch of its life. "I will never be hip enough," I announced. San Francisco Bay had a low-key pretension I didn't understand. Manhattan serves its disdain straight up. LA doesn't waste time pretending. You *are* someone. You *know* someone. Or you're *no* one. This was different.

I had to be missing something. I called my youngest sister in Miami to get her opinion. She'd lived there a long time–been on the ground floor of start-ups and penthouse of crypto. "Anna, we just drove around Marin and, well, not feeling it. Did you like it?" I asked.

She laughed. "There's a reason I left," she said, "More yoga pants than yoga mindset if you know what I mean. Too much fuss. Not enough fun. Move to Miami," she joked, "Thongs, boobs, and sunshine. The boys would love it." We were a long way from South Beach.

"Well, looks like another win for Palo Alto," I said. We stared at the bumper-to-bumper traffic ahead. The question was bigger than which town. There was no escaping the gridlock of indecision. Visiting for a weekend is one thing. Leaving family and friends over 3,000 miles away was another. How do you test-drive an entirely new life. Being a tourist is different than being a local.

"I *will* say," Gordo began, "there's a buzz out here the east coast doesn't have. Feels like the next big idea could be around any corner." He looked at me, then back at the road.

"People seem more curious about what *could be* than bracing for possible catastrophe. You know what I mean?" Gordo asked.

"Kind of," I replied. "But it also feels a bit untethered. Like a carnival tent that might pick up and be gone tomorrow." It was strange. Hard to explain. Functional, minimal, dispassionate. Billionaires in flip-flops with backpacks.

An hour later we arrived at the hotel. The air was thick with fog. A bright-eyed young valet opened the car door. "Can I get your bags," he asked enthusiastically. They were not Louis Vuitton or even leather but out there, nothing looked like everything. Wealth was wonky. We could be big investors or tech titans. Perhaps he had a great elevator pitch. Billion-dollar idea in his pocket. "We've got them, thanks," Gordo replied. We entered the lobby. It had a pricey, gray, androgenous vibe. I missed New England charm– the cozy quirkiness of our Westport home. We proceeded to reception.

"Welcome to the Marriot," the desk clerk said blankly. Her posture suggested defeat. Possible doom. Perhaps she was baffled as to how her Stanford-educated, bio-tech career had come to this. Hospitality professional. Maybe this is where dreams went to die. Fluorescent lights reflected in her eyes. *This was the part in a horror film where you just wished the couple would leave.* She confirmed our reservation. "Check-out is at nine," she said, handing us two keycards. We took them and approached the elevator.

"Hey, I made reservations at what looks like a charming Greek restaurant tonight," I said. Gordo smiled. We went to our room, called the boys to check in, showered, got dressed and drove to Taverna.

Located on a quaint neighborhood corner. Mediterranean blue doors opened into a tiny oasis of old-world charm. A beautiful young Greek woman greeted us. Her enchanting smile– a fresh start to the day. She seated us at a simple wood table. A few minutes later an older gentleman brought over three kinds of artisanal hummus plated beautifully beside warm pita. "Good evening, my name is Thanisis," he said kindly, "I am the owner. May I start with you a glass of our house wine?" he asked.

"That would be lovely, thank you," Gordo replied. "My name is Gordo, and this is my wife, Kelly." We shook hands.

"Pleasure to meet you both," he said.

"You have a beautiful restaurant, and the hostess is wonderful," I said.

"She is my daughter," he replied proudly. We drank and ate. Basked in the beauty of the moment. Shed the list of should do's and imagined the life we could build there.

The next day we drove around Palo Alto before meeting our realtor late afternoon. PALY High School looked like a sprawling resort. Town & Country mall was across the street. It felt optimistic. We met Doug, our realtor at the first house. "You must be Doug, pleasure to meet you," I said.

He looked from my Saucony sneakers to our full-size Ford Expedition rental and tried to smile. "You must be Kelly and Gordo. We have a couple great houses to see," he said with measured enthusiasm.

"Does it have air conditioning?" I asked as we approached the front door.

"It really doesn't get that hot," he replied vaguely irritated.

"Really… in August?" I confirmed.

"Maybe 80's. Open windows will provide a nice cross breeze," he assured me.

I doubted Doug got hot flashes or cared whether we melted into oblivion if we signed a lease. We toured the house to be polite. "I know you want to move quickly. Do you need to take room measurements?" he asked looking at his phone. We'd been there five minutes. I have an inner diva, brat, and oligarch. I wasn't sure which one to let out.

"That won't be necessary," I said flipping my perfectly highlighted blond hair over my shoulder. We walked down the block, passed Steve Jobs house, and arrived at a 1930's ranch with 3,000 square feet wrapped around a tiny courtyard. Small but cute and equipped with air conditioning. "Fifteen thousand a month seems a little pricey for what it is," I said to Gordo loud enough for Doug to hear.

"It sold for $7.5 million two years ago," Doug replied, unable to tolerate our insipid ignorance anther minute, "So, there is no negotiating room. In fact, the owner said there is someone else interested so if you want it, you need to let her know immediately." I turned my back to Doug. I didn't like his Gucci loafers, smug smile. or high-pressure tactics, but we didn't have another option. I'd been looking for weeks. Gordo and I walked to the car to discuss.

"Rentals in Dubai might be more. I wouldn't know. But this is insanity," I said frustrated.

"Technically, we *are* getting seven thousand for our rental at home so it's really more like eight," Gordo said. "

For a tiny ranch on a postage stamp property," I replied. We stared at the house. Good street. Good neighborhood. Good amount of charm. I could feel Doug staring at us. "He is an obsequious slug," I said.

"I know," Gordo said smiling, "Let's stay focused. I could see us here Kels." he said.

"Me too," I admitted. We walked back somewhere between excited and defeated.

"We'll take it," Gordo said.

Doug perked up a bit, "Terrific, the owner lives down the street and wants to meet you first," he said, "She's a big-time retired tech attorney so she's usually available." He stepped away to call her. Swagger in his gait. Commission on its way. Ten minutes later Shinya arrived. Doug made introductions. "I have another appointment, but I'll be in touch," he said.

Shinya was a tiny Chinese woman. She and Gordo talked crypto and the future of terrestrial-based financial markets until I thought my eyes would bleed. "Doug mentioned you are on the creative side," she said seeing my boredom, "There is a vibrant art community here. I will send you some links. There is also a fantastic farmers market, which your boys will love," she added.

"That sounds wonderful," I replied happy to be included.

She smiled at me, "Let me show you the backyard." We walked through the sliding glass door. She picked a plum from her tree and handed it to me. "Take as many as you can carry," she said. I will prepare the lease and get it to you tomorrow to sign.

"Thank you so much," I said. We raced back to the hotel to get ready for dinner with Gordo's new boss and wife.

A Red-Bearded Narcissist Delivers the Dream

Sandwiched between Posh Nail Salon and Petco was the *Odyssey Café*. Dirk had hand-picked it. We arrived early. I looked around. Maize baskets dotted pink stucco walls. Greek urns sat on cracked tile floors. Think Mexican TGI Friday on a Pier One budget. Gordo and I stared at each other. After fifteen years of marriage, some things are best left unsaid. The hostess, who looked like she'd been crying, escorted us to our table. Bad break-up? Bad boss? She wore retro platform Converse sneakers.

"Super cool kicks," I said.

She smiled at the gesture. "Thank you." She handed us menus. "Drink specials are on the back" she said, "Your server will be with you shortly."

We would have rejected *Odyssey Cafe* for the super-scripty font alone. "Dirk said this was the hottest restaurant in Palo Alto," Gordo offered. I raised my eyebrows. "Impossible to get a reservation," he added. I looked at the empty tables next to us. I was about to comment when Gordo stood up and waved. Dirk lurched toward the table, his wife behind him. There was a flurry of handshaking.

Dirk's physical appearance said it all. Darty eyes, careening posture– likely signs of underlying paranoia masked by over-bearing arrogance. Dark ginger stubble protruded from his splotchy red face– probable high blood pressure aggravated by anger issues. Mini paunch indicated long hours, fast food, and low priority on fitness. He wore a black t-shirt and misquoted Steve Jobs in the first ten minutes. Not promising. But I can be a harsh judge of character.

"The margaritas are great," he said snapping his fingers for the waitress. She came over, pad open, "Two pitchers of the Smoky Watermelon Jalapeno's," Dirk ordered, "You guys good if I order for the table?" he asked.

It was less a question than the statement of a guy who was paying for dinner. Had he seen *Wolf of Wall Street* too many times? Did he not understand wooing etiquette? I don't drink margaritas and the likelihood of me eating anything he ordered was zilch.

"Absolutely," Gordo said filling the silence. I was starving— had waited all day for this meal.

Dirk rattled off a combination of fried, cheesy, meaty options. "Jump in if there's something you want," he added. I wanted to leave. Wanted to scream. Unleash my drama queen. Instead, I channeled my best happy housewife on steroids.

"The Greek salad with grilled chicken looks ABSOLUTELY DIVINE," I declared. Gordo's half-smile begged me not to tank dinner before appetizers. Dirk studied me, unable to read my tone.

"Sure," he said tentatively to the waitress, "Let's add in a salad for the table." I was the wrong spouse for this dinner. Compliant is not in my brand character. I have a low tolerance for self-indulgent blowhards and can be inconsolably bratty if forced to eat bad food. Gordo squeezed my thigh under the table— part apology, part mercy plea. I'd try but couldn't promise anything. His wife was surprisingly dispassionate for a Mexican civil rights attorney. She spoke little. Checked her phone a couple times. Mentioned that they had a new babysitter. I figured she was just worried about childcare until Dirk spit out the story of how they met.

"You can just imagine," Dirk regaled, "Her dad was a sheriff, and I was a CEO selling *cannabis*." He leaned back tilting his head at the riveting irony. "I had to explain to him how cannabis is helping cancer patients AND how those incarcerated for possession are less likely to commit violent crimes. NOW, I was talking his language." Dirk waited for ferocious nodding, possible jaw-dropping, but I was too busy doing the math on whether Gordo had signed the contract yet and if we'd still get reimbursed for this horrible trip if we backed out.

The second I realized he was staring at me, I snapped back into the present. "Wow," I said widening my eyes in utter disbelief, shaking my head at the sheer genius– doing everything I could to reframe my delayed response as simply the dramatic reaction his spellbinding story deserved. I worried I might have overdone it, but Dirk's smug expression made it clear this was exactly what he was expecting. So, I doubled down. "That's just crazy," I said, "Did he change his mind?" I asked.

The waitress set down a platter of chili nachos. Dirk's ruddy face spread into a Cheshire cat grin revealing small yellow teeth roughly the color of corn chips. He leaned back in his chair, presenting his gloriously erect man boobs. I could feel the titillating climax was coming soon. I leaned forward intent on soaking up every inch of this unforgettable moment. Gordo slumped slightly. This was not going at all the way he expected, and we were still on appetizers.

"Nope," he said proudly. "THAT did not change his mind. He's a tough character." Dirk looked at his wife for back-up. She nodded on cue– more focused on salvaging a few chips not yet smothered by the glutenous mass of nacho cheese. "He had a bad knee, so (dramatic pause) I convinced him to try a topical for it." he said. Then, extending both hands into the air like a preacher before collection he continued, "THAT'S when he changed his mind."

I wanted to stand up and applaud. Hug him. Thank the Academy. Instead, I shook my head slowly side to side in dramatic amazement. "Well, THAT is just pure genius," I said, "So you won him over AND converted him to be a cannabis supporter." Dirk grinned, held up his right hand. At first, I thought it was a 'praise the lord' gesture. Maybe mock modesty, although that seemed unlikely. THEN, I realized he was waiting for me to high five him. It was priceless. "Yes!" I exclaimed slapping his hand like we'd just won the playoffs.

"This one's a keeper!" Dirk exclaimed looking at Gordo.

"Sure is," Gordo said flatly in total disbelief that what was happening *was* happening. I stared into Dirk's squinty eyes to see any semblance of our future. Not promising. I looked at his wife, who was checking her phone again.

"So sorry," she said to me, "Just want to make sure our babysitter is ok." I imagined the countless dinners she'd had to endure indulging strangers she'd never see again, and a husband she'd divorce as soon as his stock options vested. She wasn't dispassionate. She was exhausted. I pictured an alternate reality where she and I polished off a bottle of Pinot Noir and she told me the *real* story about how her dad threatened to shoot him with his Glock if he stepped so much as an inch out of line.

The rest of dinner flip-flopped between awkward silence and too-loud laughing. Gordo and I walked to our rental car in silence. "He seemed different at the retreat," Gordo said. I was quiet. The entertainment factor had worn off. I felt nauseous from too much cheese and the distinct feeling this might be a mistake. "I think you made him nervous," Gordo added. I shrugged. "He knew my final decision depended on you, and I don't think he could figure you out." Gordo opened my door. I got in. He got in. There was no turning back. If dinner had been the deal clincher, we would have stayed in Connecticut. I knew in my gut we'd decided long before that. Before Gordo had even negotiated the first offer. It was about more than money. More than whether I liked Dirk.

Burnout and Bloody Mary's in Half Moon Bay

Next stop: Half Moon Bay. We got up, worked-out in the hotel gym, got coffees and embarked on our afternoon getaway. A scenic thirty-minute drive through winding country roads, but my mind sped frantically through the onslaught of upcoming agenda items: *How do I register the kids for school? Was there a school bus? Were utilities included in the $15,000? Water? We still had to get renters for our Westport house which would be impossible if pool construction didn't wrap up. Should we medicate our dogs for anxiety before the flight? Was this even all worth it?*

Canna Bliss had appeared on our horizon like the archangel of hope. We'd spent a decade working at big ad agencies with big budgets and no control. Another decade running our own boutique agency with uphill battles and roller coaster returns. Gone from big potatoes to small potatoes. We needed to move beyond root vegetables. Canna Bliss felt like destiny calling. We'd finally be client-side. Calling the shots instead of scrambling to service them. We were in before we even knew what for. The money mattered. But the opportunity to launch an industry headed for the moon was irresistible. And not just any industry.

Cannabis was going to change the world. Treat depression, joint pain, PTSD and who knew what else. It had helped Gordo survive non-Hodgkin lymphoma 25 years prior to legalization. Cannabis was the all-natural non-addictive wonder drug, set to acquire the likes of Pfizer before the end of the decade. Now it's old news but then, the frenetic feeding frenzy of investors was out of control. It plastered Wall Street Journal headlines daily. Think 1990's internet explosion meets the 2007 housing market boom. No one says bubble until it pops. Cannabis was on an unprecedented trajectory.

Creative freedom. Financial windfall. Service to humanity. Most importantly the unquantifiable chance to feed our spirits and fuel our dreams. *That's* what drove us to overlook the glaring warning signs. Safety nets are key. We'd keep the agency. It had great talent and could run itself. We'd rent our house so we could return if need be. We'd move from status quo to status go. Update our vision of the future and ourselves. The situation was far from perfect. But bold opportunities don't come along every day. And *this* one absolutely had an expiration date. The meteoric rise of cannabis would not be happening twice. Caterpillars who stay in the cocoon never fly. That wouldn't be us.

We'd been driving through scrubby countryside when out of the blue a stunning castle appeared up ahead. Perched atop rugged cliffs facing the Pacific sat the Ritz Carleton at Half Moon Bay. Beauty can startle the soul. Wake it up. This would be a reset.

"I'll grab our towels if you get the water bottles," Gordo said opening the trunk. I reached into the back seat to retrieve them.

"I vote we leave all our problems in the parking lot and just soak up some sun," I suggested as I closed my door.

"Deal," Gordo replied. We navigated the winding path down to a tiny strip of coastline. Waves rose like an anthem; crashed like a blues riff. The cacophony was comforting. Hungry howling, choppy chit-chat, restless wrestle, raging roar–harmonies crisscrossed each other in a hush of halleluiah. Chorus of contradiction.

Chilly for June, I wrapped myself in a towel and sat on a large piece of driftwood. Gordo's phone buzzed. "Honey, just give me a minute. It is the relocation company," he said getting up.

"Of course," I replied, "Don't forget to ask about the dogs." The call went on for almost half an hour with Gordo pacing the thimble-size stretch of beach. My Zen turned slowly into a zoo of cagey suspicion.

He finished the call. "So, they don't handle dogs. They have two approved moving companies. We handle all details," he said.

"What about furniture rental," I asked.

"Nope," he said. We stared at the ocean. Waves crashed on the shores. "I'm sorry, Kels, this is turning into a shit-show," Gordo said. "They promised us full relocation with a point person that was supposed to handle it all. Not a list of resources we could have found ourselves."

I stood up and folded my towel, "Well, that's not very helpful," I replied irritated. The to-do list had just tripled in less than thirty minutes. We stared at each other silently. Our situation was overwhelming but neither of us had the bandwidth to solve one more problem. "I think the best course of action…" Gordo nodded ready to start tackling issues. "Is to march up to that castle and order a few Bloody Marys."

Gordo smiled. Relief in his eyes. We held hands and walked back to the hotel. I ordered my drink with extra horseradish, Gordo extra olives. We crunched down big stalks of celery. Played backgammon in front of the gas fire and reminisced about crazy boondoggles in our past until we were ready to drive back. Our flight left at nine the next morning. By the time we landed, I had a fully actionable plan.

In the car service on the way back, Gordo was glued to his phone. We flew down the Hutch at 80 mph, signs whizzing past us. Right before we merged onto the Merritt, I panicked. We were almost home to what would soon not be home. "Gordo, I need to talk with you," I said slightly panicked.

He put his phone in his pocket. "Anything," he replied.

"I know you said we'd work out the details of me launching *ETC* and running the creative department when we get there, but I need to know that's an absolute. I am giving up my career, family, and friends. I can do it if I'm working but if there's any doubt– I want to stay here with the kids. I can't be an isolated housewife in California."

Gordo grabbed my hand, "Kelly, I promise you that is the plan. I have carte blanche to run the marketing department however I see fit. We WILL do ETC, and you WILL run creative." I felt a sick sense of fledgling optimism. *That is the plan* has plans B, C and D built right in. There were no guarantees. It would be my choice.

Navigating Bi-Coastal Breakdowns with a Bucket Hat

A week later, Gordo was to fly back and set up the house. "I sent you the list for IKEA," I said mixing fresh blueberries into the muffin batter. "The kitchen list is below the furniture list." Our golden retrievers, Zezu and Floyd pranced around in circles near their food drawer. "Did anyone feed them breakfast?" I asked. Unanimous silence. Their tails wagged wildly at the word breakfast.

Gordo picked up their bowls, "I also need to register the kids for school, right," he said already exhausted at the idea of it all.

"Yes, sorry," I replied, "We tried when we were there," I reminded him, "but it had to be closer to the start date."

Luke poured himself a glass of milk. He put on a good face, but this move was his worst nightmare. "Dad there's no way you can do it all by yourself. Do you want me to come?"

Without missing a beat Gordo said, "That would be amazing." He turned to me. "What do you think?" I spread the crumble evenly over the batter.

There was no way to measure this decision. My gut instinct was that it would be a total catastrophe. His first trip there needed to be highly curated for maximum fun factors. On the other hand, it could also be an amazing bonding experience. Great opportunity for Luke to take control of the situation. I wanted to say yes. After all, the offer was kind and generous. Plus, Luke *wasn't* wrong. The task was impossible for one person. But I went with my gut. "Gordo, why don't we get you a handyman helper. I can look on Next Door," I replied.

"Sure," he said dejected.

"Mom, it's not a big deal. It will be fun. Like our lax road trips but on a plane," Luke argued. Gordo looked at me with a mix of hope, desperation, and loneliness.

"Okay," I said not at all sure it was. I put the muffins in the oven. Emotional math is futile.

Finley, Luke's 12-year-old brother was watching *The Great British Bake Off* in the adjoining family room. "Can I go," he asked jumping off the couch. Unlike Luke, he was out-of-his-mind excited for Cali– had a new surf wardrobe picked out. Was excited to be near Rodeo Drive and undaunted when we explained PA is not LA. His baseline is pure joy.

"Finley, you have the more important job," Gordo replied, "The fiberglass pool is being delivered tomorrow. I need you to help mom."

His smile turned sour, "Why doesn't Luke stay with mom if that's the more important job," he said turning our clever parenting strategies against us.

"Honey, you have an appointment with the plastic surgeon I can't cancel," I said. He had a wide scar below his left eye, the aftermath of a dog attack. It had consumed our life for two years. We didn't talk about it as much anymore, but it was always there. Lasers and steroid injections had made it less red and ropey but not less noticeable. We told him it looked like a Nike swoosh, but it made him self-conscious. "It's the only appointment they had. We need to see if the scar has healed enough for us to get revisionary surgery when we're home at Christmas," I reminded him.

"Luke gets to have all the fun," he said plopping back on the couch for The Show Stopper finale.

"We are going to have ten times more fun than them," I said.

"Yeah," Luke said, "Mom will probably take you to Terrain for one of your fancy lunch dates." Finley flipped him off.

Two days later Gordo and Luke were setting up our new life in Palo Alto. Finley and I held our breath as the 20 by 40 fiberglass pool bladder was hoisted like a beached whale above our new neighbor's recently paved driveway. Voluminous amounts of water cascaded out. "I am so sorry," I said to the mom, who was furiously pacing, while talking on the phone. I prayed the cookies I'd delivered when they moved in would buy me a little leeway. An hour later the pool had made it up our driveway and was hovering above the giant hole in our backyard. Several neighbors and their children had gathered to watch. Finley stood by my side taking in the spectacle.

They were lowering the pulleys when one slipped, and the giant fiberglass shell fell– landing with a thunderous splintering crack. The neighbors' eyes widened followed by audible gasps. They turned to me, then to the foreman as he walked over to inspect it. "It's fine," he announced. "No damage. We were almost there anyway."

My eyes filled up. Finley squeezed my hand. "It's okay mom," he said quietly.

It wasn't. None of it was. "I am going inside," I said in my most light-hearted way to our neighbors. I called Gordo in tears.

"Can I call you back?" he asked.

"No. The pool cracked… I feel like everything is cracking… including me," I said crying.

"So is Luke," Gordo said. I stopped crying instantly.

"What happened," I asked.

"The school registration lady was a bitch. It's not going well," he whispered, "He is crying. I need to call you back."

I sank to the floor. "Okay," I said, "I love you. Please tell Luke I love him."

Finley came in and sat beside me. "The guy told me there was a small crack, but they would fix it," he said. I began crying harder. "We can fix this," Finley said putting his arm around me.

"I'm sorry sweetheart, Luke isn't doing well. School thing did not go well. This is beginning to feel like a nightmare. I'm just hoping this isn't all a big mistake." My mind twisted with mistakes. We should have gone with gunite. We should have gone to set up the house as a family. We should have gone with a whole different plan.

"Mom, you remember what you told me after the dog attack?" Finley asked.

I looked at him and smiled, "That it's not what happens to us but how we let it shape us," I said.

"Maybe that's the same thing with this," he said. Smart boy. We talked for a while. Afterward, Finley went to play basketball at the beach with his friends and I packed for a couple hours. Then, flat-out exhausted I facetimed my friend Dante.

We'd met ten years earlier when I was working on my second album. Dante came highly recommended from a friend who owned a music studio in New York. I wasn't looking to be a rock star. Lyrics just came through me, and I wanted to give them a voice. He was perfect– a down-to-earth diva with high standards and kind eyes. He pulled notes out of me I didn't know I had. Connected my voice to my heart in a way that made the lyrics come to life. We became dear friends. He was frequently on tour with Billy Joel or Stevie Wonder, so it was a longshot he'd be there, but after two rings his big, black, beautiful face filled my screen. "Hello!" he exclaimed with his signature booming enthusiasm.

"What continent am I reaching you on," I asked delighted to see his face.

"Doing a sound check in Japan. Perfect timing," he said.

"What hotshot are you touring with this time," I asked.

"Who cares, I have the queen on the phone. I want to talk to *her*," he said.

Queen. I hadn't felt like a queen in a long time. I began to cry. "Sorry Dante," I said, "I can call you back later."

"Nope," he said. "Now is good. What's going on," he asked. "A million things really. I guess at the heart of it I just feel– like nothing matters. I don't know what the point of anything is. Especially this move," I said.

"What if there is no point?" he asked.

I laughed. "Well, that's not the *go out there and get 'em* pep talk I was expecting.

"I'm serious," Dante said. "What if none of it ever amounts to anything? Would you still do it?" he asked. We were quiet for a minute. Something in me settled. "Kind of takes the pressure off, right? Then it just comes down to what your heart wants. What direction your spirit wants to go." We talked a while longer about his multiple boyfriends and fancy new foot massager.

When we hung up, I saw Gordo's text– a picture of Luke wearing an Ikea bucket hat holding up a Costco palette of cinnamon buns in one hand giving a thumbs up with the other. Gordo's note: *This stupid bucket hat has saved us.* I wept. Lifeboats show up in strange ways.

The last week went by in a blink. Our friends Zoe and Charlie threw us a beautiful good-bye beach bash. Spectacular sunset. Robust cheese platter. Chilled Sancerre. "We want to give you a little going away present," Zoe said handing me a gift bag filled with Westport themed stationary, notepads, and a framed picture of all of us taken at my birthday. "The boys have something for Luke," she added. Luke's friends handed him an oversized fleece picture blanket filled with shots of all the great times they'd had together.

A bubble of joy before the two-day tornado of preparation. I was excited to take-off. Terrified to land. I felt like a David Letterman guest waiting in the Green Room before stepping on stage. High anxiety. Pukey excitement. August 1st, we left the house at 3am. I looked back before shutting the door. What were we doing? Ripping our happy kids from their beautiful home? Leaving it to renters we'd never met. I was flooded with guilt and regret. Then, with one thick thud, I closed that chapter of our lives.

PART TWO:

WELCOME TO WONDERLAND

Greeted by Shrieking Goats and a Gadfly

We got into an oversized SUV with 2 dogs, 2 crates, 2 children and Julio, the driver who'd taken us to and from adventures on four continents. This would be a one-way trip. We drove in silence. Luke was on his phone. "Honey, who are you texting this early," I asked.

"I'm not texting anyone. I'm changing my screensaver to a 365-day countdown," he replied. We'd had the *It's important to step into this new adventure* talk ad nauseum. We'd also promised to come home in a year if it wasn't working.

We arrived at JFK terminal ARK Pet Oasis. "Luke, will you and Dad assemble the crates," I said, "Finley and I will stay with the dogs." Zezu and Floyd were shaking, scared. We petted them. Promised it would be okay. Just a plane ride.

"Guys you can't stick your head out the window," Finley said trying to lighten the mood. We weren't allowed to medicate them. They needed to be alert in case of emergency. We'd tried acclimating them to the crates with no luck. Luke and Gordo pushed and shoved them inside as they twisted and contorted themselves. Finally, after the metal latches were locked, they paced and whimpered. Gordo petted them through the bars. I muscled through tears pretending to organize our luggage. We stopped in the food court for crap pancakes and boarded the plane. Halfway into our flight, I broke down in the bathroom. I knew where we'd left. I had no idea where we were going.

We arrived. Got our big ass Suburban. Picked up the dogs. Drove to our new address on Washington Avenue in Palo Alto. Thanks to Gordo and Luke's whirlwind shopping efforts, we had couches, beds, and a Costco-size tray of cinnamon buns. The movers had already come so we had clothes and enough knickknacks to feel like home. My friend Samantha stopped by with everything from paper towels to kale salad and chocolate chip cookies. She was a red-headed fireplug and the recruiter who'd introduced Gordo to Dirk. We'd barely said hello when there was a loud knock at the door. I opened it.

"Hi, my name is Virginia Samson. That's S-A-M-S-O-N," she said, "I borrowed your composting garbage and noticed when you were here last week you did not separate recycling properly. Clear bags for plastic. Cans and bottles separate. Do not mix them with composting. Palo Alto is very serious about this," she said. Gordo and Finley joined us. She continued, "What are all your names. Say them slowly and spell them please."

Gordo squeezed my hand. *She inspected our garbage bins? Seriously?* I looked around to see if she had a loaf of banana bread, small fern– or any semblance of house-warming gift. Nope. I spelled our names– some twice because I spoke too fast. "My daughter lives with me. She will be your son's 7th grade English teacher." Finley's eyes widened. She peered past us to get a look at Luke who had not come to the door. "Okay then, I'll return the bins when I'm done."

Gordo closed the door. "Okay then," he said.

We sat back down with Sam. She told us about all the nearby cool hiking. Gave Gordo a few updates about new Canna Bliss hires. We devoured the food. After she left, we unpacked for a few hours. As I transferred my last box of hanging clothes onto the closet bar, it ripped from the wall and crashed to the ground.

Sundresses collided into flannels in a heap of plaster. I looked through the now giant hole into the hallway.

Finley walked by and waved. "Oops," he said.

I burst out laughing. Absurdity is liberating. "Let's blow this popsicle stand," I said, "Get Daddy and your brother. We need a break." I'd heard a lot about the Stanford Mall. Chockful of high-end stores like Pink Berry, Tesla, Apple, and Nintendo. Enough distractions to temporarily drown out the drama of moving. We piled into the car leaving a mountainous heap of cardboard boxes in the driveway. I fully expected Virginia to have called the garbage police by the time we got back.

Not all malls are created equal. In New England, even upscale malls feel like a claustrophobic retail maze with windowless food courts that smell of fried food and body odor. The Stanford Mall on the other hand is a breath-taking botanical garden of beautiful shops. Wide outdoor stone walkways punctuated by cascading planters and open-air fireplaces. A haven for butterflies, birds, and brilliant Stanford students. Every few yards there's elegant seating– with cushions, that apparently no one steals. Endless opportunities to have a smoothie after soul cycle or debate the attributes of Metallic Midnight for your new Model X– all while enjoying the soothing sound of spa music. We strolled around for a while, eyes like saucers, until Gordo spotted the Tesla store. Tesla is everywhere now, but back in 2018, only the very hippest on the east coast had them. We'd certainly never been to a dealer.

"You guys want to check out the Tesla store," Gordo asked.

"Absolutely," Finley said, "Are we getting one?"

I grabbed his hand while we were walking, "Maybe two," I said jokingly.

"Excellent," Finley replied, "Let's definitely get one with the scissor doors." We entered. After a couple minutes a sales guy came over and addressed Luke and Finley.

"Do you guys want to get in," he asked.

"Sure, thanks," Luke said sitting on the passenger side. The sales guy opened the driver door for Finley. He slid in.

"Can you show me how to make the turn signal fart," he asked. I looked at Gordo confused.

"Sure," the sales guy said. "You want the horn to sound like shrieking goats and change the map to Mars?"

Finley's eyes lit up. "Definitely," he said. Within seconds he had the Tesla in Santa mode. The car icon became a sleigh pulled by two reindeer with light-up collars. He clicked the blinker, and it played jingle bells.

"My name is Derrick, you are welcome to take it out for a day gratis," he said handing Gordo a business card.

"That is super nice. We will be back," Gordo replied. Even Luke, who was committed to hating California got into the driver's seat of the Model X and took a selfie. Gordo looked at me excited. I could feel him ready to blurt out something about how much Luke was going to love California if he just gave it a chance. I grabbed his hand, squeezed it, and discreetly shook my head *no*. We walked out.

"I need a frozen yogurt," I said, "Let's go to Pink Berry." We all got a large yogurt with toppings and sat on the nearby couch.

"That was pretty cool," Luke said. I smiled at Gordo. He nodded. Small win. Worth the wait. We ate our yogurts, explored some other stores, and headed to the car.

"I want to stop at Equinox on the way back," I said, "It's supposed to have a rooftop pool. I pictured Gordo and I having coffee poolside after early morning workouts. Ten minutes later, we pulled into an industrial parking lot. Across the street was a McDonalds and Sal's Tech Repair.

"Not promising," Gordo said.

"Probably just understated from the outside," I relied, "You guys want to come in," I asked the boys.

"We'll wait in the car," Luke replied. Gordo and I got out. Entered the gym. The interior was concrete minimalism. More prison than sanctuary. The snack bar was limited. Metal seats discouraged lounge time.

"Can I help you?" asked a young woman behind the steel reception desk. Her tone hovered between suspicion and contempt.

"Um, yes, we are thinking about joining and wanted to get a quick tour," I said.

"Our sales manager is out till Tuesday," she said, "I can set up an appointment then." *Three-day wait?* Was I in an alternate universe? Health clubs usually stalk you. Snubbing is not really a membership strategy.

"Okay, but we were thinking of joining sooner," I said, "Could we show ourselves around if we promise not to be long?" I asked.

"Hold on," she said irritated, "I'll get Jonathon." She disappeared behind the desk. "Should be a fun tour," Gordo said. Jonathon came out in slim-fit, ankle-exposed black pants and wire-rim glasses.

"Hi, I'm sorry but I only have a few minutes," he said stepping from behind the desk to shake our hands. "This is the lift area," he said gesturing left, "And the spin room," he said gesturing right. "You are welcome to look around the locker rooms. The lap pool is accessible from outside," he said handing Gordo his business card, "Let me know if I can be of further assistance." The locker rooms were cramped. The pool was surrounded by parking lots. Disappointment for double the cost.

Pitching Paradise with Fat Black Crows

Cut-throat realtor meets cruise director. That was my role week one. Plaster on the smile and sell the California Dream. How tough could it be? It was California. We'd been the year before. Had breakfast in Santa Monica at Shutters. Done pull-ups at Muscle Beach. Walked Rodeo Drove and watched Finley try on fur coats at Louis Vuitton. We drove to Big Sur. Had lunch at Sierra Mar. Tried beekeeping at Carmel Valley Ranch. Hiked at Pebble Beach. Devoured sour dough chowder bowls at the Wharf and wandered Ghirardelli Square. They loved it.

How different could Silicon Valley be? I pitched Stanford fields like it was the French Riviera. Dropped them off to play lacrosse. Went home to unpack. My new neighbor Lisa met me in the street as I pulled up. Warmth exploded from her small body.

"We are so glad you're here. You must take the boys and dogs to the Baylands. And if you like hiking, we can do The Dish. Dave and I would love to throw a welcome party so you can meet some people on the block," she said. Her eyes were playful, yet alert. I felt my face soften.

"That would be wonderful. So generous. Thank you," I said, "And we'd love to have you over once we get settled," I added. I had a friend. Maybe this was all going to be ok.

I powered through a bunch of kitchen boxes, then drove back to pick up the boys– excited to hear how it went. They got up from the curb and walked to the car. "No lacrosse nets, so we just passed for a while." Luke said.

"Oh no, did I drop you at the wrong field?" I asked.

"No, they don't have one. Lacrosse is not a big thing here," Luke said. Ugh. Not a perfect start.

"Tomorrow, we surf in Santa Cruz," I exclaimed.

"Awesome," Finley replied. Luke was silent. Hard to sell a wombat on the attributes of daylight. "You guys want to get lunch and go shopping at Town & Country," I asked.

"Absolutely," Finley said.

"Sure," Luke added. We had tacos and ice cream. Then went home to unpack.

That evening, Lisa stopped by with her husband Dave. "Where abouts on the east coast are you from?" he asked.

"Town called Westport," Gordo said.

"Is that near Greenwich?" Dave asked.

"Not far," I said.

"We have a good friend who moved here from there. I'll introduce you." Dave replied. He talked to the boys about lacrosse and how they felt about the move. "If you guys are around this weekend, I'll take you to Mike's Diner. It's where all the big tech deals go down," he said.

Lisa chimed in, "They have to try the shakes at Milk Bar," she said. "Absolutely," Dave confirmed, "Best in town."

High tide in Santa Cruz wasn't until midday so I went for a run. Kipling Street dead-ended into Homer one block from the park. Coleridge intersected Emerson before the Whole Foods and Melville ran parallel to Whitman. I listened for poetry through the pavement. Nothing but the sound of my own heavy breathing. Five miles later I felt no different. No endorphin high. No new perspective on life. The homes were charming. Landscape beautifully maintained. But something was missing. There was an unnerving predictability about the city grid structure. Highly functional. Short on whimsy. No rocky coastline or meandering stone walls. No cute burrowing chipmunks. Just the occasional black squirrel. I stopped in front of our house to stretch. Fat black crows congregated in the street. They cackled like old women with apocalyptic prophesies.

Gordo was at work, but the boys were ready to go when I returned. We drove half an hour south, paid the parking meter and rented wetsuits at the SUP Shack. Their instructor, Sam, led us across the street and down the beach. "Should be some good waves today," he said, "nothing too crazy. We're going to stay in the center guys, okay, cause the waves break close to the rocks on the far side."

Luke and Finley nodded, "Okay," they replied. We got to the right spot and into the water they went. I sat on my towel to watch them. Within minutes I was surrounded by swarms of tiny black biting bugs. I swatted them. Wrapped myself in the towel.

"Punkies," said a dude heading out with his board, "that's what we call them. It's better in the water but you need a suit." *Great,* I thought. I wrapped myself up like a mummy.

"The midges *are* nasty today," a woman said sitting near me.

"Not what I was expecting," I said smiling.

"Humidity makes them worse," she replied.

Punkie biting midges. Delightful.

I walked back to the parking lot, sat on a fire hydrant, and called our attorney for an update on the lawsuit regarding Finley's dog attack. It had been going on for two and a half years. A dog belonging to a friend of Finley's had brutally attacked him in the face. Horrifying but we assumed we'd figure it out amicably, until, Nora, the mom, said Finley had tormented her dog and it was only acting in self-defense. I'd witnessed the whole thing. Seen her walk back to the kitchen after opening the door. Seen Finley bend down to pet her dog. Watched as it lurched toward his face, latch onto it and not let go. I couldn't imagine the kind-hearted Nora I'd come to know accusing a victimized child of something he didn't do. She had gone out of her way to welcome us to Westport. Set up get togethers to introduce Finley and I to all her friends. It was deeply troubling. We did not want to sue, but they claimed no liability and we had a mountain of bills.

Teachers, friends, family– people we barely knew had written letters on his behalf saying what a sweet, good-natured, dog-loving boy he was. I wanted to ask our attorney if they'd made a difference, but his secretary said he was in court, so I left a message. Next, I texted my sister Tina to see how my nana was doing. She had early onset dementia. We were trying to get her into an assisted living facility but the one only one she liked was full. I also left a message for the head coach of West Coast Stars to check on club lacrosse tryouts for Luke. An hour later, I fed the parking meter enough quarters to get us through lunch and batted my way back through biting midges to take shots of the boys surfing– capture this picture-perfect memory forever.

We ate sweaty nachos at the beach cafe, purchased cheesy t-shirts, and drove home. Halfway there, Finley asked, "Was that the right Santa Cruz?" Luke and I laughed.

"I know. I'm sorry. I kind of thought it would be…"

Luke chimed in, "Hip, cool or fun," he suggested.

"Yeah, kind of," I replied, "It's no Nantucket." I felt like a traitor to sunshine. Like a New England curmudgeon at a hippie throwback festival. I don't fit neatly many places. I've tried.

If Only the Assassins Guild Served Cookies

The fourth day of school. Finley went to Bobo's after last period with his new friend Oscar. He refused to be defined by his dog attack. Kids *did* ask about the scar, but they thought it was cool. Saw it as bragging rights. It no longer shut him down. Nothing did. He'd seized the opportunity to reinvent himself. Show his quirky, fun, lovable side. Classmates were drawn to him. He was drawn to the lifestyle. Unlike at home, kids in Palo Alto biked everywhere. It filled him with freedom. Autonomy. School-night, dinner times had become an afterthought. I was mixing pesto into a large bowl of rigatoni when the screen door flew open. I looked at the clock. Too early to be Finley.

"There will not be a second day of soccer try-outs," Luke announced as he threw his backpack on the couch.

"What do you mean," I asked.

"Let's just say it was a bad idea. The only kid worse than me was vaping on the way to the field," Luke said. He opened and closed the fridge. Took nothing out.

"But you are so fast and strong and athletic," I said.

"Like I said yesterday, most of these kids have been playing since before they could walk. Dribbling, passing, trapping– they are *actual skills*." He opened and closed cabinets.

"I got goldfish. They're underneath." I said,

"It was totally humiliating," he added.

"I'm sorry," I replied. Then trying to lighten the mood, I added, "You could always go back to water polo?" He'd tried it in middle school and hated it. Wasn't a fan of pruned skin, toe-nail scratching, or treading water.

"It's fine," he said, "I will wait till lacrosse starts." Luke opened the Costco container of goldfish and poured a thousand or so into a salad bowl.

"Five months of *Fortnite* is not an option," I said, "If you don't plug into something, you will never make friends."

He threw up a goldfish– caught it in his mouth. "And the problem with that is?" Luke asked.

"Okay then, looks like we are moving on to Plan B," I said, "Tomorrow's the last day you can join an after-school club so don't come home until you have. You aren't sitting in your bedroom until spring."

He took the bowl. "There are no clubs," he mumbled on his way out.

"That's impossible," I said.

The next day at 10:30 a.m. he texted: *Look for yourself. Do you want me to join Cookies and Miracles or The Assassins Guild?* I looked it up. *Um, ok. You are right. Sorry.* I texted back. What kind of school didn't have newspaper or yearbook? He replied: *Maybe if they had Cookies and Assassins...* I didn't have a Plan C. Weeks passed. Each day felt like an eternity. Grit and gusto weren't going to cut it. Finley loved life but hated school. Luke hated all of it. Gordo left early each morning. Got lost coming home each night. Despite GPS. Canna Bliss culture was different than advertised. Dirk turned out to be a raging psychopath. Demanded someone's cock on the block daily. Threatened mass firings. Hours were 24/7. Failure to reply to a 3 a.m. text resulted in public ridicule the next day in status. The insanity was nonstop.

I had shelved my own career until the craziness died down. But it appeared to be chronic, not acute. I had not signed up to be a California house-mom. The solitude was making me stir-crazy, and the monotony left me depressed. Usually, I have no problem asserting my needs, but the situation had become complicated. Our destiny felt like it was spinning out of control. Gordo was rarely present even when he was. The six foot, two inch Renaissance man who laughed easily, played football with the boys, and never missed a date night was never home. Succeeding at his job had become an unwinnable proposition. Gordo could always figure out anything– fix a car. Play guitar. Design a house, logo, or killer business plan. He'd survived an embezzling business partner and cancer, but this was different. Dirk thrived off chaos. He was a bombastic bully and an energy vampire.

Gordo's unshakable confidence had been shaken. It wasn't his fault my job was still on hold, but my patience was wearing thin. The move was hard on all of us. I needed him to follow through on Dirk's promise. So, early one morning before Gordo left for work, I confronted him.

"What is going on with my creative director job AND the *ETC* program?" I asked. "You promised that was part of this deal." Gordo was silent. "I need that to happen now," I said.

"You're right Kelly. And I'm sorry. I am doing everything I can. I promise you it will. We just need to get through this next round of funding," he replied looking at his watch.

The pit in my stomach hardened. "Which will be when?" I asked.

"Soon," Gordo replied checking his phone, "Soon." I could tell he was nervous about being late. With Dirk minutes mattered. He kissed me goodbye. I watched him peel down the driveway. Next rounds have a way of going around and around.

I grew up with deals that were always just about to close. My dad forever on the brink of a break-through; my mom perpetually on the verge of a break-down. Lies are toxic. But truth is not absolute. I felt angry, betrayed, and hopeless. But so did Gordo. He needed me to believe things would work out. So did the boys. In fairness, I didn't know they wouldn't. I tried not to let doubt consume me. I looked for freelance work, but Silicon Valley prefers algorithms to creative campaigns. I tried to write poetry, essays, lyrics– anything, but my mind was a maze. The house had become a U-shaped hallway with waiting rooms at either end. I wandered from the bedroom to the kitchen and back. Felt isolated and alone. Cried. Got to the gym. Got groceries. I got it all done but it was getting me down. My sisters and friends checked in. They meant well but their optimism felt obtuse. I was drowning. I didn't need love. I needed a lifeline.

Distraction was the next best thing. I was in a deep thicket of thoughts when my phone rang. "You up to hike the Dish," Lisa asked. \

"Sure am," I replied.

"See you in a sec," she responded. Lisa called regularly to go on life-saving hikes. A few minutes later we met outside. "Long or short loop?" she asked as we got into her Mission Leaf.

"Think I need a long loop this morning," I said.

Her husband Dave drove a Chevy Volt. It was the west-coast version of New England tycoons driving vintage Volvos. Made me smile. "Me too," Lisa replied.

"Need to climb some real hills," I replied laughing. We parked and walked to the gate. The entry sign cautioned walkers to: *Watch out for rattlesnakes, mountain lions, and black bears.* I noticed it each time we went but something that morning made me stop. "Has anyone actually been attacked," I asked.

"Actually, there was a woman last year who…" she stopped herself, and opened the gate for me, "Well, that was an unusual situation because she was here after dark," she reassured me.

"Comforting," I joked. We power hiked up hills, past fields of cattle and panoramic views of The Bay. Objectively beautiful, but I preferred New England with its red barns and meandering farms. We talked about everything from AstroTurf lawns to the best roasted nuts at Trader Joe's to the spike in local teenage suicides.

"They've actually had to put up fences around the train tracks," Lisa said.

"That is terrible. Must be a lot of pressure for kids with the bar set so high. I've never felt *that* dire, but I've definitely been in dark places," I responded.

"Me too, I had a lot of trouble in school. Got good grades but always felt overwhelmed," Lisa replied.

"How funny," I said, "I had the same issue. Studied ten times harder than the other kids for the same results. I remember going in for extra help in Algebra. When I didn't understand, he just yelled the same instruction louder."

Lisa laughed, "As it you had a hearing problem," she said, "Imagine anyone thinking there might be *a reason* for that." Lisa shook her head at the absurdity. I wasn't quite sure what she meant by *reason*. "Even these days," she continued, "schools rarely consider that girls could have ADHD. Thankfully, when our daughter Abbey was struggling, her counselor suggested we get her tested. She asked if Dave or I had it since it can be hereditary. I told her neither of us had any symptoms. She said it presents differently in girls and women. Asked if I'd struggled in school or ever resorted to substances to cope."

We passed the big satellite dish. I kicked a stone in the path. Debated how much to share, "That is fascinating," I said, "I never used substances, but I did have a serious eating disorder– only thing I could control."

Lisa chimed in right away, "I drank my way through high school AND college. People saw me as a party girl but it's the only time I really felt happy," she said.

"So did you get tested?" I asked.

"Yes. It was liberating. All this time, I'd thought there was something wrong with me. Truth is, I have ADHD. There's an on-line test I can send if you want," Lisa offered.

"That would be great," I replied, "Finley has it– so maybe I do too." We rounded the last bend in our hike. "We've been treating it with diet and exercise, but middle school is proving impossible for him," I said.

Lisa nodded, "That's right around the time Abbey started taking medication. She couldn't have survived school without it. I take it too– not all the time but it helps me cut through the static. Allows me to focus on one thing at a time." We approached the car. Lisa opened her door. Unlocked mine.

That afternoon, I took the on-line test. Dove deep into the ADHD rabbit hole. Researched every article I could find. It opened my eyes. Like someone holding up a mirror to my brain– pointing out what I'd labeled flaws were merely different ways a mind can work. Not shortcomings I needed to cover up. I was shocked no therapist I'd ever seen had thought to explore this option. It provided explanations for so many things I'd thought were my fault. I wasn't stupid or inept. I had ADHD. I met Finley after school, and we walked home together. "I want to ask you about something," I said, "I was talking with Lisa today. Her daughter Abbey has ADHD and said medication helped a lot. Especially in school."

Finley stopped and looked at me. "You said we would never resort to that," he reminded me defensively.

I nodded. "You're right but I read something this afternoon that changed my mind," I said.

Finley readjusted his backpack. "I will raise my grades, okay," he said.

"I don't care about your grades," I said, "Let's sit down for a minute." I plunked myself on some nearby wood chips. Finley sat beside me. "You wouldn't deny someone who had Diabetes insulin right?" Finley shook his head no. "You wouldn't tell them to just tough it out or work harder to get through it."

Finley's eyes filled up. I held his hand. "It's the same with ADHD. It's not about trying harder or eating better or exercising more. Your brain, and today I learned mine too, is wired differently."

Finley looked at me surprised. "You have it too," he asked.

"Yes, I always thought I just wasn't as smart as other kids."

Finley interrupted, "But you are," he said.

"And so are you," I replied. "Medication doesn't change *what* you think. It just helps with *how*– clears up the traffic jam of thoughts. Makes them go single file. At least that's what I read. I'm going to try it. You don't have to. It's totally your call," I said.

"Let's do it together," he said. We met with his new pediatrician. Lisa introduced me to a doctor who diagnosed me and by week's end we were both on Vyvanse. Over the next few weeks, Finley's grades moved from Ds to Bs. More importantly, he said he didn't feel *left behind* anymore. It helped me feel less overwhelmed, but my issues were situational. I still felt stuck.

Sampling Plumcots with Hairy-Toed Men

We had a long, narrow driveway with a fence on one side, spikey rose bushes on the other and a detached garage at the far end filled with empty packing boxes. I rummaged through them for helmets. Luke sat on his bike, helmet dangling from his handlebars, eyes glued to his phone. He was wearing a grey t-shirt, grey lacrosse shorts and grey sneakers. Low-key prison-wear. Gordo emptied the contents of a backpack. I wheeled my bike out of the garage with a ski helmet on my head. Luke looked up, "You're wearing *that?*" he asked.

"Oh, I'm sorry Mister *Daddy found everything I need so I could scroll TikTok.* Yes, I am, as there doesn't appear to be another *bike* helmet and I can't deal with Finley lecturing me about why he must wear one if I'm not. Unless of course... *you* want to wear it?"

Luke flashed a teethy smile, "I'm good. Thanks."

If Finley had a signature song it would be Bruno Mars, *24 karat Magic*. His entrances are epic. Ever since he was little, he's had a singularly unique style. The back screen door swung open, and he emerged. His bright yellow Human Race sneakers landed on the rotting baseboard. Tight white t-shirt tucked into slim-fit Adidas trackpants. Bright floral baseball cap with white framed sunglasses and my Louis Vuitton backpack slung over his shoulder. Luke looked up. Shook his head. This is where the soundtrack, if there was one, would shift into *It's the End of the World as We Know It,* by R.E.M.

Luke rolled his eyes, "Tell me, you are *not* wearing *that,*" he said.

Finley didn't miss a beat. "At least I am not wearing a Groutfit," he replied.

I looked at Luke confused. "Grey. Outfit. Groutfit," he said flatly.

"Has anyone seen the first aid kit?" Gordo asked.

"Dad, seriously, we are going to the *Farmers Market*," Luke said.

"With helmets on," Finley added.

"Do you want me to look for the kneepads," I joked.

"Very funny," Gordo replied pulling it out of a stray backpack. "You'll thank me one day." We exited the driveway and headed down Washington Avenue.

Finley took the lead. "Make a left," he yelled back hitting play on his phone. Frank Sinatra's *New York, New York* played before kicking into *Empire State of Mind*. I bopped my ski helmet side to side; Finley leaned back gangster-style– arms in the air. Mortified, Luke rode on the far sidewalk.

"One hand on the bike, *please* Finley," Gordo shouted from behind. We parked at the bike racks, locked them up and walked arm-in-arm through the California Street Tunnel. It was no *Hollywood Hills Swingers* scene, but it *was* a moment.

Vendors lined the street. Gordo turned to the boys, "Who wants an egg sandwich?" he asked standing in front of the first food truck.

"I do," said Finley.

"No thanks," Luke replied.

"Luke and I are going to go check things out," I said. We passed an old guy playing John Denver's *Country Roads*. Next to him a tattooed dude was twisting balloons into alligators and giraffes. "You want a pretty pink Poodle," I asked Luke.

"How about a nice big middle finger," he replied lovingly.

We passed a variety of food vendors. "Seriously honey," I said, "You're going to be hungry later. Why don't you get something to eat. It *is* a farmer's market."

Luke looked at two nearby stands, "Umm, I'm not totally in the mood for spicy tabouli bowls or gluten-free squash muffins."

I looked around, "What about some nice spinach nan with pickled radish tapenade?" He smiled. I stopped at a fruit vendor and tried a plumcot sample. "Delicious," I exclaimed offering Luke a slice. He gestured to the man's Birkenstock's beside us– white hairy toes splayed out over the edges. "Thanks," I said cringing.

Luke held up a deferential hand. "Not a problem," he replied, "That's why I'm here." We passed a roasted nut booth. I tried six or seven. Some twice. Luke nudged me. "I think you need to buy something, or we need to go," he whispered.

I smiled sheepishly at the vendor. "We'll be back," I said.

"Can I have some money for Subway," Luke asked pointing to the big yellow sign across the street. I gave him a twenty.

To the right was a store called Zombie Runner. "I'll be next door," I said. "Lisa told me they have a cult following." I entered. On one side was a line of people waiting for gourmet coffee. On the other– a wall of high-end sneakers and OOFOS. I picked one off the wall.

"They absorb 37% more impact than foam recovery footwear," the salesguy said.

"Sounds great," I replied. "I'll try a size 7."

Gordo entered with both boys. "Best egg sammie I've ever had," Finley said.

"Nothing compared to this meatball parm," Luke replied holding up his Subway bag like a trophy.

The salesguy returned with my size. I tried them on while Gordo and Finley ordered coffee beverages. "Like stepping on clouds," I said, "I'll take them." I paid.

Finley returned with a tower of whipped cream. "The iced peppermint oat milk latte is delicious. Want a sip," he offered.

"Too rich for my blood," I said jokingly.

Gordo smiled, "I got us a cold brew nitro."

Luke cracked open his Mountain Dew, flipping off the whole health-nut, comfy-shoe culture. Small rebellions are essential for survival. We finished walking through the market. Finley ate every non-GMO nutbar, drank all 12 samples of fruit-infused frozen lemonades and got curried hummus to go. He *loved* it all. Luke loved the endless opportunity for sarcastic commentary. We crossed back under the tunnel laughing until our stomachs hurt. Finley and I held hands on the bike ride back. Gordo snapped a picture.

Entering a Sri Lankan Temple and Pigeon Pose

"I can't believe we still haven't seen each other. Can you come Sunday afternoon for a swim with the boys," Gabby said.

"Perfect," I replied, "Can't wait to see you AND meet John!" Gabby and I had met ten years before at a Wake-Up Festival in Colorado. We'd practiced Quantum Consciousness, Energy Tapping, Red Hot Yoga and Radical Mindfulness. Shared our lives over a French rosé by the firepit. I knew little about her day-to-day life. Just that she was a seeker like me who'd been a nurse before meeting her husband.

She said he travelled a lot for board meetings and surf trips, so she'd raised their five children mostly on her own. But now they were grown so she had time to attend things like Angel Whispering Seminars and Witch trainings. I was riveted. People I knew participated in book clubs and pickle-ball tournaments. Not spellcasting and tarot-card reading. I fell in love. We kept in touch. Talked every few months. Sent notes and gifts. She lived in a town called Atherton, which meant nothing to me until Sunday afternoon.

We parked in a shallow driveway. Walked around the path to a charming house. The pool was centered on a big lawn next to a stunning mansion next door. Gabby greeted us, "Oh my gosh," she said hugging me and shaking the boys' hands, "It is SO nice to meet you all. I have been hearing about you for years." Gordo and the boys introduced themselves. Finley plucked a strawberry off the beautiful fruit platter. "I wasn't sure what kind of snacks you boys like, but the guest house is stocked, so help yourself. And there's soda and seltzer in the pool house. *Guest house... pool house?* "Want a quick tour," she asked the boys.

"Definitely," Finley said.

"That would be great," Luke added. I am just going to let John know you all are here," she said. As if on cue he walked across the yard.

"Hello," he greeted us, "Sorry I was in the wood shop," he said dusting off his shorts.

"John is building a beautiful dining room table for our house in Laguna" Gabby said, "Honey, do you want to give the tour? You're better at it than I am."

John took over the tour. "Well, you've seen the pool house. This is the guest house where our kids stay when they come home." He opened the slider to reveal a two-story fireplace with spiral staircases on either side and a gourmet kitchen outfitted with custom retro mint-colored appliances.

Julie offered the boys cookies. "We designed it like a 1950's Lakehouse. Thought it would be fun for the kids," she said. Luke looked at me, raised his eyebrows.

"There's two bedrooms on each side," John said gesturing to the upstairs as we exited the cottage. "And that is the gym," he continued, pointing to the full weight room visible behind glass-garage doors. "Back here," he said as we snaked around a crop of tropical trees, "is the authentic Sri Lankan temple I gave Gabby for her 50th. We had it dismantled in Anuradhapura and reassembled here."

Luke and Finley climbed inside. "You are welcome to come play in it anytime," Gabby said.

"Wow," Finley exclaimed exiting, "This is incredible. Do you have ceremonies?" he asked.

"Not in a long time– But I did," she added not wanting Finley to think it was just for show. "Maybe we'll have one," she suggested.

"That would be awesome," he replied.

"I'd love to see the wood shop," Gordo mentioned looking at the building ahead. He and Finley had built our barn doors and coffee table. We passed three garages and entered a building roughly the size of our first floor at home. Every drawer was meticulously labeled. There were multiple steel sawhorses with benches and laser cutters. Gordo walked over to the full bar with a 60-inch tv behind it. "You must spend a lot of time out here," he said.

John gestured to the office, "That's where I do CAD drawings for the small-scale models before I start a project. Make sure I work out all the details first." I almost burst out laughing. We have more of a *measure twice, cut-once* and return to Home Depot when it doesn't work philosophy. "And a kitchen," John continued as we passed it, "with a bathroom because once I start a project I don't like to stop."

Gordo nodded in amazement, "I mean you could live out here," he said.

"Sometimes he does," Gabby commented half-laughing.

"Some guys play tennis. I do this," John responded. There were several active projects including a ten-foot blond balsam wood table. Gordo ran in his fingers over it. "Had the wood sent from Costa Rica," John said.

"Beautiful," Gordo replied. The boys were standing stick straight near the door. The workshop had a distinctly museum-like vibe– nothing was meant to be touched.

"This must be boring for the boys," Gabby said apologetically, "Do you guys like cars," she asked.

"Love them," Finley said. He smiled at me. I could tell he'd be willing to be adopted if the topic came up. This was much closer to the lifestyle he imagined for himself. We walked over to the first garage.

"Do you like Ferraris," John asked the boys.

"More a fan of old Porsches," Gordo replied. I could tell he was tiring of *show-and-tell*.

"I love Ferrari's," Finley said.

"Well, we've got both," John replied opening the first 6-car garage with his phone. "That's an F-40," he said to Finley pointing to the one and half million-dollar cherry red car in front.

"Wow," Finley whispered mesmerized by it all.

Gordo headed to the back of the garage. "That 66' Alfa Romeo Duetto Spider is the best car here," he said. Gordo didn't care about the glitz. He wanted to know if John was a legitimate car guy. Enthusiast or poser. John followed him back. Gordo admired the Spider from every angle. "Sexier than Ms. Robinson, right," he said.

"Best character in *The Graduate*," John said appreciating Gordo's reference. "It's my favorite car to drive," he added.

Gordo smiled. "When it's on the road," he remarked.

John laughed. "So true. I got sick of having it in the shop but couldn't bring myself to sell it." They talked about cars. First cars. Clunkers. Dream cars. Best movie cars. Over a five-course meal of car talk, they moved from tolerated husbands to early-stage acquaintances.

Gabby and I migrated back to the pool with the boys. She brought out two giant mermaid tails. "I know these are super girlsy, but I bought them for one of my daughter's birthdays in high school. Might be fun," she said holding them out to the boys.

"No thanks," Luke politely declined.

"Why not," Finley exclaimed. He put one on, dove in, and swam around. Gabby and I caught up on our lives. She heated up the sauna and steam. The boys went from one to the other and back to the pool. They got chips from the guest house, sodas from the pool house, lifted weights in the gym. Best time EVER. She offered them huge chocolate chip cookies for the car ride home.

I googled Atherton on our way back. "Apparently it's the wealthiest suburb in America," I said.

"What gave it away," Luke joked.

"They are so nice AND interesting," Finley said.

"This is the best cookie I've ever had," Luke commented, taking the last bite. We drove back to the rental. Chatted about cars and mermaids and temples. Shared our favorite parts of the afternoon. We turned onto Washington Avenue and the fun began to fade. Gordo pulled into the narrow driveway. Parked beside the dying rose bush. The magic crashed to a halt. Our reality was decidedly less romantic. It wasn't that I wanted what Gabby had. Well, maybe just the guest cottage and gym. I wasn't jealous of her money. I was jealous of her joy. I didn't want *her* home, but I did want to feel *at* home. Gabby seemed happy. I felt like a tired hummingbird in a flowerless land.

The next day was 82 degrees and sunny. Just like the past 28 days. It required an unreasonable level of positivity. "Another beautiful day," Gordo said with deflated enthusiasm. I longed for thunder to express my rage. Lightning to illuminate our fractured reality.

"Is it ever going to rain," Luke asked. I wanted permission to sit on the couch with a vat of popcorn and watch movies. Instead, I crossed the street to Lisa's for a backyard yoga class. I'm not great at holding anything for very long– smiles, grudges, or downward dog. I'm more comfortable with high intensity cardio than peaceful warrior. But I hoped to make a few friends, perhaps get some insight into the high school scene.

"Kelly, I want you to meet Sienna," Lisa said.

She turned to Sienna, "Kelly and her family just moved in across the street."

Sienna shook my hand. "Welcome to the neighborhood," she said, "What do you do?" It was an innocent enough question. My mind raced… *What did I used to do? What do I actually do? What do I wish I did?*

"Right now, it's a full-time job just finding doctors and getting the kids settled," I joked.

The woman next to her responded, "Happy to give you recommendations if you need any," she offered.

"That would be great. Thank you," I replied.

They unrolled their mats. Updated each other on pro-bono diversity cases, LGBTQ counseling, and marathon-training. I opted not to share my insights on cauliflower-crusted pizza and tubular mascara. *What* you say frames *who* you are, and I wasn't sure yet who I wanted to be in this new world. Listening beats blabbing. Plus, the energy was invigorating. Lisa's backyard buzzed with possibility. Thinking was in. Status was out. They didn't care about looks or money. The currency was ideas. Status came from what you did, not what you had.

Sienna began. "Good morning. Today, as we move through the poses let's see where they take us. Put your hands on your heart. Take a deep breath in." We swept through sun salutations. The AstroTurf grass felt stiff to my feet. We slipped into crow pose, one position where I felt confident. I leaned forward. Touched my chest to the ground. Sienna adjusted my back right leg to be even with my hip. "You are very flexible," she whispered kindly. She pressed down gently to deepen the stretch. Tears popped out of my eyes and fell down my cheeks. "You okay," she asked. I nodded. It didn't hurt. I wasn't sure why I was crying. "It is a deeply opening position," she said. "See where it takes you. You're doing great." She moved on to help the others. We ended in savasana with namaste. I felt stressed out and stupid.

Capping Off Chaos with Nuclear Orange Parasites

It had been a long week. The Specialized Mountain bike Luke rode to school was stolen because he forgot to lock it. I wanted to lecture him about responsibility, but his eyes were hollow. His spirit seemed broken. "Don't worry about it. You can use my bike. Just lock it okay," I said.

"I'll walk, but thanks," he replied. My bike was light blue with a slanted bar. He felt judged already. I got it. He'd left tons of friends who loved him in a town where lacrosse was king. We were living in upside down world. He didn't play the right sport, wear the right clothes, or have the right vibe.

"I love you Luke," I said. It was all I had.

The next day my car got rear-ended in Trader Joe's parking lot. To round things out, Friday afternoon, there was a knock on our door. I opened it. "Hi, we haven't met yet. I am Sharon, Finley's English teacher. I live across the street. I believe you met my mom, Virginia," she said sternly. Pinpricks of heat exploded all over my body. Her tone was chiding– same as her mom's. Empty hands suggested she didn't have a housewarming gift either. My first instinct was to scream or head-butt her or slam the door.

I smiled tersely, "Yes, your mom stopped by when we moved in." I studied her. Sensible haircut. Vegan shoes. Trousers likely made from hemp, bamboo, or recycled plastic.

"Your son Finley refuses to properly edit his work." She waited for my horrified response. I wanted to hug her. Jump for joy. That meant he was actually *doing* it. Surprised by my silence, she continued, "Nor has he turned in any homework at all for the past two weeks. This is becoming a flagrant problem," she informed me, her shifty ferret eyes scanning the house behind me.

Flagrant problem seemed a bit overstated. Problem, sure. Flagrant seemed more suited for aggressive sports fouls. She didn't look like she watched a lot of NFL. We had an ex-pediatrician like her once. His response to hearing Finley had lit a candle without permission, was to warn us he'd likely be a future arsonist if we didn't put him in psychotherapy immediately. I shut down Sharon the same way I had to him, "Thank you so much for this valuable information and your genuine concern." I stepped back to close the door.

She stepped closer. "I just don't want to see him go down a bad path," she continued, "He is not taking responsibility. I have seen this type of behavior before." She went on to enumerate a well-articulated variety of future potential catastrophes.

I wondered how she'd survived growing up with Virginia. Probably not a lot of dance parties and sock puppets. "Anyway, I have papers to grade. I just thought you should know. He is welcome to come over after school if he wants to and I can help him," she said.

I almost burst out laughing. "That is a great idea," I replied.

She looked surprised and a little nervous. "I can't do it tonight but any other time," she added.

"He will be so happy to hear that," I replied.

She nodded. "I just don't want to see him fail," she paused, "Well, continue to fail," she corrected herself.

"Thank you for this illuminating update. Have a lovely night Sharon," I said and closed the door. I watched her walk down our path. Door-to-door proselytizing was the domain of Mormon missionaries. Not teacher conferences. All teacher conferences back-home began with how much they loved Finley. How he was the only student that asked about their day. The only student that made them music playlists. Even in second grade when Ms. Malkin had to ask Finley to refrain from telling Jada Pinkett to *shut her pie hole,* she admitted thinking it was funny and *did* mention that Jada tended to be a bossy-pants loudmouth.

That night, I shared the surprise visitor with Finley. "Guess who stopped by today," I said.

"No idea," Finley responded.

"Your English teacher. She was so concerned she came to the house," I said. Finley rolled his eyes. I continued, "She said you have a slew of unedited papers and two weeks of overdue homework." Finley was silent. "Are you having trouble focusing? You *are* taking the ADHD pills, right?" I asked. More silence. "Finley, this is the part where you tell me what's going on," I said.

"Coach wants me to bulk up and they kill my appetite," he said.

"Seriously?" I asked, "It's after-school touch football. Is that not a little overkill?" Finley looked at me flatly. "Ugh. Okay," I agreed, "I will schedule talk to your doctor a different medication, but until then can you just eat breakfast before and take them?" I asked. He nodded. "She offered to have you do your homework at her house if it helps," I said smiling. He quickly shook his head no. "Just know that option is out there," I said teasingly.

Gordo came home unusually early with a bouquet of bombshells. "Dirk retracted everything not written into our contract. Flat-out no new hires. No new office location. He cut the marketing budget in half so I cannot hire you to be the creative director," he said.

"What about ETC," I asked. Gordo closed his eyes embarrassed to relay what must have been a humiliating conversation.

"Dirk said it was a bonehead waste of money and the stupidest idea he'd ever heard. I'm so sorry," Gordo apologized.

"Well, he didn't mince words," I said sitting down.

"I don't know what to say," Gordo replied, "I never would have taken this job had I known any of this. I'm so sorry." My west coast career was over before it began. I was deflated but not surprised.

I wanted to be angry, but Gordo's eyes were full of something I hadn't seen before. Defeat. Luke's too. Even Finley's enthusiasm had faded with school challenges. We'd always done hard things together but slowly we'd grown apart– begun living separate lives. Each of us trapped in a world the rest of us couldn't see. We shared meals and love, but our experiences were impossible to explain. Personal silos where we struggled to survive. I couldn't change the challenges, but that Saturday morning, I decided to change the scenery. "Hey, Lisa has been telling me about the Baylands. She says it's beautiful. I thought we'd switch it up this morning. Take Zezu and Floyd for a walk there. What do you guys think?" I asked.

Luke laid down on the couch. "I'm kind of tired. Can we just make pancakes," he said.

"Nope, "I responded, "We need to shift up the energy. Let's go. I'll put the dogs in the car." Fifteen minutes later, we pulled into the parking lot. Garbage cans lined the perimeter.

"Beautiful," Luke said sarcastically. We exited the car, and I pulled him aside,

"Please no more snarky comments. I get it," I said, "I'm the first one to be sarcastic, but I'm trying really hard to make this new life we have okay." I unexpectedly broke down. "Even though none of us are, even though we never should have moved here, I just need the next hour to be okay."

Luke gave me a hug. "I'm sorry Mama," he said, "I totally understand."

We walked the labyrinth of trails. Marsh bogs flanked either side. "It looks like Mars," Finley said.

"Super cool," Luke added sincerely trying to be positive.

I put my arm around him, "Thank you for loving my swamp outing," I said.

"I love *you* and it's a beautiful swamp," Luke replied putting his arm around me too. Nuclear-orange foliage grew along the perimeter.

"Kind of looks like petrified angel hair pasta covered in Cheetoh powder," Gordo said. I googled it when we got home. *Dodder, a parasitic plant that grows on Pickleweed, blocking out its sunlight and eventually strangling it to death.*

Sunday night Lisa and Dave threw us a welcome party. Luke stayed for an obligatory hour. Finley chatted up a movie producer about the best Yeezy rip-off sites. Sharon and I avoided each other. Gordo connected with a Long Island transplant about the best old-school bars in Manhattan. Later he talked to Dave privately. "We visited a friend of Kelly's last weekend who lives in Atherton," Gordo said, "I don't know what I failed to do in MY career but that is a wholly other world. Everything out here is," he said.

Dave laughed. "Don't let any of these people fool you," he said, "They aren't geniuses. They just lived in the right zip code at the right time. All you had to do out here was breathe during the tech boom and you made millions," he said.

Lisa introduced me to a friend who'd moved from Greenwich, "Susan, this is Kelly. She and her family just moved out here. You and Tim have been here for what… two years?" Lisa asked.

"It's been three now. Hard to believe," Susan said. "First year was tough, but now we love it." Three years was an eternity. I had no idea how we'd make it three months.

"Did the kids like it," I asked.

"Hated it. Our older daughter wouldn't come out of her room for months. But now she is on the water polo team and has really embraced it," Susan said.

"I'm not sure my older son is going to make it that long," I said half-joking. "He'll be fine. Just takes some adjusting," Susan replied.

I smiled politely. "What brought you out here?" I asked.

"Tim and I both took work sabbaticals to be Stanford interns.

"That sounds fascinating. How does it work?" I asked.

"Stanford has a year-long leadership program for executives looking to change the world through innovation. There are people in film, finance, technology– all different backgrounds," she said.

"What a great experience," I said.

"We loved it," she replied, "so when they asked if we wanted to stay and continue our project, we said yes."

Perhaps I'd apply. I tried to think of what I could do to change the world. Mostly, I just wanted to change into my pj's. But maybe it wasn't as grandiose as I imagined. "What was your project?" I asked.

"It's called The Hunger Project. The platform is to end poverty and hunger by pioneering sustainable, grassroots, women-centered strategies. My initiative is to scale global production for low-cost biodegradable bags, so dried goods don't spoil. We just got back from Kenya. It's a long haul but we're making progress," she said.

Hmmm... Progress. My current definition was not having a breakdown before noon.

Part Three:

Escape from Hell

Towering Inferno of Beef and Tijuana Black Box

Assimilate. Acclimate. Adapt. That was our plan. Hard to execute without tools. So, despite forbidding the boys to play football growing up, we caved in the hopes it would help Luke find friends. Fear of depression superseded risk of concussion. We were late to the season, but the coach gave him permission to join the team. Luke's athleticism would likely compensate for his lack of experience. Plus, he was a quick study and hard worker. He'd pick it up quickly– hopefully along with a few new buddies. We'd been on the sports circuit long enough to know that parents who get involved have kids who get accepted. So, when the opportunity arose to volunteer, I signed us both up. I'd work the snack bar, Gordo the grill. *This* is where it was going to all come together. We'd socialize, meet sports parents– get the lay of the land. Do a little networking magic. Nonchalantly amass some new friends.

The night before there was a 9th grade parents get-together at the high school. A couple blocks before we arrived Gordo slowed down. "Hey, I have a great idea. What about I take you to that delicious Greek place and we skip this thing," he said.

"Not a chance," I replied, "I don't want to go either but if we're forcing Luke to try, we can't very well bail." We pulled into the parking lot. A sea of strangers mingled on the school field. "Forty-five minutes," I said dreading it. We got out of the car.

"Deal," Gordo replied. We milled around. Most parents were excitedly catching up on their summers. We didn't want to be the newbie losers.

After wandering around for a while, we found a stray couple near the gymnasium and introduced ourselves. Peter and

Sofi. I repeated it in my head. Tried to commit it to memory. "How is your ninth grader liking school," I asked.

"She was out last year doing an immersion program at M.I.T. We spent the summer in Europe with family, so she's trying to reconnect with old friends," Sofi said. She had a lilting Italian accent and sky-blue linen scarf wrapped around her slender shoulders. Understatedly sophisticated.

"What a great experience that must have been. She must be very smart," I responded.

Sofi smiled disarmingly. "We have no idea where she gets it from."

Her husband chimed in, "Certainly not us," he said laughing.

They were probably both geniuses. They asked about 'our student'. We told them about Luke. Our move. His lacrosse talent. The challenges of being new in town. We exchanged numbers, said we should get together, and parted ways. It hadn't been half an hour, but we were done. It felt like we were treading water in a pool of Olympic swimmers. We headed back to the parking lot.

"Hello there," a voice said. I turned around. Standing behind us was the couple from Greenwich doing their *Change the World* internship at Stanford. "I never got to hear about what brought you and your husband out here. What do *you* do?" she asked. Genuine curiosity in her voice. It was a simple question. I looked at the World Wildlife Federation reusable water bottle in her hand and took a sip of my diet coke. Debated whether to tell her about the poetry award I'd won in high school or burst into tears.

"It's been quite a full-time job trying to get settled here," I said.

"It absolutely is," she agreed emphatically.

"But you did that AND worked," I replied with just a hint of defeat.

"Failed miserably at both," she said, "It's fine now but was anything but for the first six months. You'll figure it out," she assured me.

I told her about the albums I'd written and recorded, the books I'd published, my career in advertising and the ETC program I hoped to launch. "That is just amazing. I don't have a creative bone in my body. I wish I could do all that," she said.

I laughed. "I'm doing a whole lot of nothing at this moment. But thank you."

The next day was Friday night lights. We arrived early for our shifts. I entered the snack shack, introduced myself and got to work. Stacked chips on shelves, poured lard into the popcorn maker, emptied cheese pouches for nachos. Shelly, a senior's mom, explained the cashbox, credit card machine and price structure. "Cheetos go quickly so if you need to restock, they're in back," she said.

"Orange sodas too. If you run out let me know and I'll grab another case," a second mom added.

"Thank you. We're new so it's my first time doing this. Grateful for the help," I said.

Shelly pulled down a box from the top shelf marked Lay's and handed it to me, "Welcome! It's a great group. Your son is going to love it," she assured me.

I took the box, sliced it open and started stocking shelves. I liked having a job– being useful. I'd dazzle them with my customer service savvy and transactional speed. Solidify my value as a team mom. Things went smoothly at first. Then, I started getting return customers complaining they still didn't have their hamburger. They'd pay me, then take the receipt to the grill to collect their burger. "I'm so sorry," I'd say. "I can give you your money back. Not sure what is going on. Maybe give it a few more minutes." My stomach churned. Gordo was on grill.

Turned out, Gordo's grill partner, Larry was not a grill master. He greeted Gordo in a *Kiss the Chef* apron and leather loafers. "I've never worked the grill," Larry told him.

"It's pretty easy– Probably the same as your grill at home," Gordo responded.

"No, I mean I've never worked *any* grill," Larry replied.

Gordo got things going. Tried to hide his shock that a grown man had failed to ever work a grill.

"How long have you been married," Larry asked.

"You want to keep the heat high to get a nice sear on the outside, flip them after a few minutes so they don't burn," Gordo said ignoring the question.

Larry nodded standing to the side. "Do you have intercourse often?" he asked.

Gordo ripped open a sleeve of buns.

"They say physical intimacy diminishes over time," Larry added.

"Hey, Larry can you hand me a stack of patties from the cooler," Gordo said.

"Sure, where is it," Larry asked.

Gordo studied him for a moment. Dull stare. Slow-motion movements. He was either on the spectrum, bullied into volunteering by his wife or an emotional zombie. "They are behind you," Gordo said. Larry snapped into action like a sloth on Thorazine. The odds he had a healthy sex life were low.

Gordo's phone had been blowing up. Once the grill was running smoothly and people were getting their burgers, he excused himself for a minute. "Larry, I've got to take this. Just flip them in a few minutes. I won't be long, okay," Gordo said. Larry gave him the thumbs up.

One of your company's cannabis delivery drivers has been kidnapped. The GPS black box puts the car in Tijuana before it goes dark. The text was from an unknown number. Gordo called it. "This is the San Jose Sheriff. We have your number as an officer of Canna Bliss. The first two contacts on the list were unreachable. How much cash and marijuana were in the car?" he asked.

Gordo paused. Managing international narcotic felony crimes was not in his job description. "I am new to the company," Gordo said exuding his best *calm in crisis* demeanor. "Can I call our director of operations and get right back to you?" he said.

"We will probably need you to come in. Be on alert. We'll call back when we've learned more," the Sheriff replied.

Gordo discovered three things. One. This had happened a couple times before. Two. If it didn't get resolved quickly, the FBI would be involved. Three. Legal counsel needed to be notified immediately. He should not answer ANY questions. He did as he was directed. When he turned around the grill was a towering inferno of beef.

"Larry!" Gordo yelled, "What happened?" Gordo tried to close the lid without being consumed by flames.

Larry stood back holding his spatula like a scene from *American Gothic*. "I don't know. It just kind of blew up," he said.

Gordo reopened the grill. Grease splattered up at his face. Thick black smoke permeated his new PALY sweatshirt. "How can I help," Larry asked after the smoke had cleared.

"My shift's over," Gordo said, "Good luck." Gordo came to get me. We skipped the game and headed home.

"Looks like grill duty was a big success," I said sarcastically.

Gordo attempted to wipe the grease from his glasses. "Long story," he replied.

"Chilidogs were a big hit," I reported. "As was I," I added jokingly. Gordo didn't break a smile. "Seriously, the moms were super nice. How about the dads?" I asked.

Gordo raised his eyebrows. "Not big grillers," he said. Halfway home his phone buzzed. He pushed answer on the car screen. Held up his index finger for me to be quiet.

"Hello this is the San Jose Sheriff calling back." I stared at Gordo terrified. "We suspect foul play. The car was burned. Cash box is gone. Looks like an inside job. No need to come in," he said.

"Thank you so much officer," Gordo replied. He hung up. We looked at each other. "That's only the half of it," Gordo said, "My new friend Larry asked about our sex life."

Larry. Virginia. Dirk. Sharon. Silicon Valley culture was indeed curious. Mad Hatters and Queens of Hearts disguised as tech moguls and neighbors.

Fire-eating Goblins and a Sky Full of Drones

October 31st is like a sacred holiday in Old Palo Alto. Tech billionaires take Halloween very seriously. Lisa strongly recommended checking out the set construction mid-afternoon before the crowds arrived. I had no idea what she meant but agreed to go. That morning Luke woke up feeling too *sick* to go to school. I missed 3 months of school in 7th grade for the same kind of *sickness*. "Maybe lunch in Los Gatos would help," I offered smiling.

"I think so," he replied appreciatively.

"Chicken wings and a chocolate milkshake should cure you," I said, "We just need to get back early enough to see what this town does for Halloween. Lisa said it's bigger than Christmas."

Lunch was bland and expensive but the people watching was priceless. An older woman sat at the bar sipping a Cosmo. She looked at her Chanel handbag sitting on the barstool next to her. "Mama's going to by you some pretty barrettes today," she promised her perfectly coiffed Shih Tzu as she gently pushing the bangs out of its eyes.

"Why does she look so puffy," Luke whispered to me.

"The dog or the woman?" I asked.

"Very funny, the woman," Luke replied.

"Too much filler," I said, "She's trying to inject her way back to thirty, but her clinician got a little too ambitious. "More importantly, what is her dog thinking?" I asked.

"*I can't move,*" Luke said in a high-pitched voice, "*I just want to be walked like the other dogs. Please Mama! Please!*"

I laughed, "I don't know, I think inside that bag are tiny little pedicured paws that can't bear to touch pavement. I think there's a spoiled power brat in there." Then in my very best Veruca Salt voice, from *Willy Wonka*, I said, "*Mother, I want a diamond-studded collar. Not just any collar. A diamond collar. I want it NOW.* We imagined full backstories for the two men sharing a plate of fried calamari and the waitress frantically texting in the back corner. I picked at an overdressed salad. Luke ate a few bites of his overcooked burger and we left.

My disgust for synthetic cobwebs, witches stuck to trees and blow-up ghosts is likely inherited from my mother. What we returned to was not even a distant relative of the Halloween I'd come to hate. Steve Jobs wife had a full team of carpenters and stagehands setting up a block-long lil' shop of horrors town. The lot across the street had legitimate trapeze artists somersaulted through midair. There were fire-eating goblins and twelve-foot clowns rehearsing. Life-size cotton candy machines spinning. A full-blown spooky circus.

We ran into Lisa a block from our house. "Crazy, right" she said.

"Mind-blowing," I replied, "Never seen anything like it."

She gave us VIP wristbands for the nine-piece Motown band performing later. Early that evening, Gordo took Finley trick-or-treating. One house was giving out ten-pound Nestle bars. Another– laptops to the first twenty children. Lines snaked for blocks. Streets crawled with kids hopped up on sugar and greed– like a scene from *Charlie and the Chocolate Factory*. Lisa and I boogied down with the Motown band. Luke played *Fortnite* in his room with kids from home.

A few nights later I was sitting on the couch polishing off a pint of mint frozen yogurt when the sky lit up. It looked like fireworks, but it wasn't New Year's or Fourth of July. "Gordo, come here," I said leaning forward but not getting up. "Do you see that?" He opened the sliding door and went outside. It sounded like a swarm of angry wasps were descending on the house.

"What the… Boys, we're going out front. Kels, get up. It's crazy. I don't know what this is." We walked out front. The streets filled with neighbors. Lisa and Dave came out of their house. There was an eerie feeling in the air.

Great, I thought, *this is the part of where we all get abducted by aliens who force us to harvest plutonium from precarious cliffs without harnessing gear.* "What *is* that?" I asked.

"I think it's coming from Larry Paige's house," Dave said. We walked to the end of the block. Stared at the sky. It lit up with hearts that turned into confetti. Dave spoke with a few neighbors and reported back. "What do you get for the woman who has it all on her birthday? A five-hundred-drone show."

Lisa looked at Dave, "My birthday's coming up," she joked.

"You don't have everything yet," he said smiling.

The next day, Lisa phoned to see if I wanted to pick figs with her at an older couples house a few doors down. "Absolutely," I replied. "Fresh figs… yes please!" Lisa noted they were very particular, so to make sure I followed their directions.

Sounded odd, but having experienced Virginia our first day, nothing was shocking. We knocked. The husband answered. Looked at us skeptically.

"Mira suggested we come by to pick figs," Lisa said smiling. He furrowed his brow. "But we can come back another time if now is not good," she added.

Mira poked her head out. "It's okay, I said they could come," she confirmed. Lisa introduced me. Mira exited the house, took us into the back yard. "Over here," she said. We followed obediently. "You can pick from *this* branch or *this* one," she said gesturing to two. "*Those* are ripe. Do *not* pull hard." Lisa and I gingerly plucked one after another. "Go ahead, try one," Mira demanded. We did.

"Wow, they are delicious," I said.

Mira was pleased. "Where do you live?" she asked me.

Lisa answered, "Across the street from us. They moved in about a month ago."

Mira's husband's face lit up with excitement, "Do you live next to those horrible new people who run their air conditioner all time of the day and night?" he asked.

Lisa smiled at me discreetly and shrugged apologetically. I debated whether to be flabbergasted that anyone would care so little about the environment but decided to go for dead-pan honesty. "We *are* those neighbors," I said picking another fig.

"Oh, sorry," he said, "I just don't know why you'd need to run it so much." I considered sharing my chronic hot flashes and rejection of estrogen replacement therapy for fear of dying of breast cancer like my mom. Or sharing with him that the white noise helps me sleep through the depression moving to this godforsaken town has caused. I opted to go with the advice of Gordo's first mentor. *Never underestimate the opportunity not to say a bloody thing.*

After a few minutes of awkwardness, Lisa saved us. "This is so kind of you. Thank you," she said.

I walked over to each of them and shook hands, "This is my first time picking fresh figs. I appreciate your generosity."

Mira nodded nervously, "Yes, yes," she said, seeming a little unsettled by her husband's earlier comment. "Well, hopefully we will see you again," she added. Her husband grunted something close to goodbye and opened the gate for us to leave.

"It was a pleasure to meet you both," I said. Lisa and I left. Remained silent until we were out of earshot. Laughed the rest of the way home.

That night Gordo and I met Gabby and her husband for dinner across the street from their house at the Menlo Circus Club. "This is beautiful," I said as the hostess dropped us at their table.

"It is an equestrian club," John said standing up to say hello.

"Do you all ride a lot?" I asked.

"No," Gabby laughed, "Actually not at all, "But it was fun when the kids were little. There's pool and tennis and they could just walk here." she said.

A young waitress took our drink orders. "Lot of Stanford students work here," John added after she'd left.

"Great place to meet future employers," I replied. John smiled and nodded.

"Kelly used to ride," Gordo said, "You did the show circuit, right honey?"

Gordo loved to dramatically overstate my riding career so he could watch me wiggle my way out of it. "Show circuit might be a stretch," I said smiling, "My sisters and I rode when we were younger. Hunter class mostly. My little sister did make it to Madison Square Garden though," I added proudly.

"That is amazing," Gabby replied. Your parents must have been so proud." The waitress delivered our drinks. "How are the boys doing?" she asked.

"Good," I said, "Well, mostly," I corrected myself, "Luke had quite a scare yesterday. They had a lockdown at the school. There was a gunman on campus."

Gordo looked at me shocked, "WHAT," he said.

"I'm sorry," I said awkwardly apologizing, "You got home from work after I'd gone to bed," I explained.

"Success doesn't happen staying at home, right," John said.

Gordo ignored him. "What happened?" he asked me.

"The school had a lockdown, but since it's an open campus, Luke was outside between classes. He saw the guy. The guy looked directly at him and held the gun in front of his lips signaling him not to scream," I said. My insides shook thinking about it again. Gordo stared silently at his vodka tonic.

"That is terrifying," Gabby said, "I'm so sorry." She reached out to hold my hand.

Embarrassed, I said, "No, no, I'm sorry, this is not dinner conversation."

Gabby reached for a bag by her feet and handed it to me. "This hardly makes up for that, but I did get the boys a little something," she said.

"That is so sweet of you. I'm pretty sure they'd like you to adopt them," I added trying to lighten the mood.

Gordo phoned it in for the rest of dinner. "I'm sorry for not telling you earlier," I said on the way home.

"I am never home," he said angrily. "John may see it as badge of honor. I don't. I hate it. I hate all of this. We define success very differently," he said.

"I think he was just trying to make you feel better about the situation," I replied. "He was trying to make his wife feel better about missing their kids' childhoods," Gordo retorted. I wasn't sure what to say. Choices require sacrifice. Everyone does the best they can.

"I'm sorry, I love you," I said holding his hand. We arrived home and the boys opened Gabby's gifts. Brand-new set of Apple AirPods Max. They were over the moon.

Choosing Electric Bikes over Adult Diapers

Do you feel settled yet? Zoe texted early one morning. A seemingly innocuous question. I looked out the vertical blinds in our bedroom at the yellow grass and burst into tears. The night tables Gordo and Finley put together looked like they belonged in a doll's house. The kitchen drawers stuck. The front door was impossible to open. Our bedroom was dark even with the lights on. Sure, we had purchased a deluxe five-star Cuisinart toaster, an adjustable silverware tray, and cozy chenille throws. But it all felt like a stage set. We'd settled our *stuff* but not our *selves*. The temporariness felt terminal.

Finley yelled from the kitchen, "Mom, can you check my word problems before I go to school." I walked in and set my coffee on the table. Finley handed me his homework and ate a bite of waffles.

Luke plunked down and reached for the maple syrup. The table shifted. My coffee spilled all over Finley's math sheets. "Dude," Finley yelled, "Are you mentally challenged. You know the table is broken," he said throwing his arms up in anger. I dried the coffee with paper towels.

"Everything here is broken," Luke snapped back. He grabbed his backpack and left.

"I'm sorry Finley. We will figure this out," I said running out to catch Luke before he was gone. "Wait," I said as he started to bike down the driveway. "It wasn't your fault. Wayfair is sending the missing part to fix the table."

He tried to slink by the rose bush to avoid hitting the car. Scratched his arm. "What about all the other parts," he snapped.

He reached the street and stopped. Looked back at me, "I'm sorry Mom, I love you," he said.

"I love you too honey," I replied, "Can I get you a Band-Aid?" I asked.

"No thanks," he said and rode away– leaving the house he hated to go to the school he hated more. I cried in the driveway. Rewrote Finley's math paper while he got dressed. It wasn't one thing. It was everything. We'd tried to settle in– visited the Baylands, the Farmer's Market, and the Dish. Volunteered at the football game, eaten at every restaurant in town. We'd tried to grow roots, but mostly we just kept busy. School, work, grocery shopping, dog-walking, house-cleaning, laundry. It all had an uneasy flatness about it.

Then one Sunday afternoon, Luke and Finley were throwing a football to each other in the backyard. I was flipping through a J. Crew catalogue. "Tomorrow starts school spirit week," Luke said, "Can I stay home? Monday's theme is *Dress Like a Baby*." I cringed.

"Are you going to," I asked.

"Not a chance," Luke said.

"Isn't that a little– awkward– and kind of lame?" I asked.

"Ya think," Luke responded. Finley threw a high spiral. It sailed over Luke's head and crashed through the floor-to-ceiling plate glass living room window.

"Seriously," I said to Finley.

"It was an accident," he said.

"It was," Luke responded, nervous I'd go ballistic.

"They're less likely to happen if you're careful," I said frustrated.

Luke dropped the football– returned to his signature sullen state. "I'm sorry," he said, "We'll clean it up." He and Finley went into the house to get garbage bags. I couldn't take any more. There was no room to move. No room for error. We were lions living in cages. Fireflies trapped in jars.

"Both of you come back here right now," I yelled. I picked up the football. Handed it to Finley. "We live in a doll's house with a crap backyard surrounded by glass windows. See if you can break the rest. We can't live anymore in fear of every stupid little thing." They looked at me shocked. Nervously smiled. "Play ball," I announced sipping my lime seltzer, ignoring the shards of smashed glass surrounding me.

"You heard her Finley," Luke said. The game continued. Defiance surged through my veins. I ripped through catalogue pages.

"If you change your mind, Luke, I can go to our third world CVS and pick up a baby rattle and nice pair of Adult Diapers," I offered.

"Tempting, but I'll pass," Luke said laughing. There was a glimmer of my old Luke. I wanted him back full-time. Wanted our old life back.

"I have a great idea. Let's rent electric bikes tomorrow– ride them across the Golden Gate," I said.

"Hold up," Luke said, waiting to throw the football. "What about school?" he asked.

"If you'd rather go to school, that's okay," I said.

"No, no, no," Finley said terrified the offer would be retracted.

"All good to cut school," Luke confirmed.

They both came over and sat next to me. "Well, you wouldn't be cutting school if you were," I coughed a few times, "sick," I finished.

"Can dad come?" Finley asked.

"Work is very stressful for him right now," Luke said, "So, probably not, but we can ask." He looked at me hopefully.

"Absolutely," I said, knowing there was zero chance. I could feel my energy and optimism returning. I researched our outing all evening. We'd rent bikes at Fisherman's Wharf– electric for them. Old school for me. Fresh air. New sites. Wide open space. No rules. It would be good for our spirits.

Next morning, we set off. The boys were out-of-their-mind excited to be getting e-bikes. They rode no hands– fast as the wind. Finley fell, scraped his knee, got up laughing. "If dad was here, we'd have a first aid kit," he said smiling. We soaked in the sun, stopped at the Art Palace, coasted past Crissy Field, peed at the Warming Hut after which Finley guilted me into buying a cheesy overpriced golden gate keyring for Gordo. We took pictures at Fort Point and rode over the Golden Gate– Alcatraz in the distance. We opted against biking into Sausalito in favor of returning for lunch at Smith & Wollensky's.

Luke let me test-drive his e-bike on the way back. "So much power," I said flying past him.

"It's awesome right," he said catching up.

"Totally," I said slowing down to give it back.

"You can keep it mom. I'm okay," he said. He looked at me with such joy, such pure generosity– it almost made my heart burst. Strange how love can be so beautiful and painful all at once. The car ride home hummed with happiness– everyone yammering on about their favorite parts until both boys fell asleep. Bliss.

Child Services, Shotguns, and a Jumbo Popcorn

Several days later Luke came home and handed me a letter from Palo Alto High School. "They are mailing a copy as well," he said. The letter informed us he'd missed 25% of school. We needed to call to explain the absences and if he missed anymore Child Services would be getting involved.

"That's ridiculous, you have definitely not missed that much school," I said.

"That's what I thought too, but we have had eighty days and I've missed twenty," he said. I paused, a little dumbfounded. Thinking back, it *was* possible.

"Oops," I said raising my eyebrows, "Not good. No more mental health days I guess," I said. The next day I called the school.

"Don't worry," the attendance lady told me, "They must send that note out by law. I know Luke has had a tough adjustment," she said. "He eats lunch with me sometimes. It can be a tough place to fit in. He is a sweet boy."

My eyes filled with tears. "Thank you for taking care of him," I said trying to keep my voice steady, "I can't tell you how much that means." We hung up. How would I give Luke relief with my number one strategy kiboshed? I had no clue.

Our life went quickly from falling apart to a freight train of catastrophe. Gordo got blindsided by a car running a red light. He called me stunned and disoriented. "Are you okay?" I asked.

"Yes, pretty sore and stiff but nothing broken," he replied.

"I am so sorry honey. How about the car?" I asked.

"Totaled," he said. "I'm going to uber home after I fill out the police report." Dave was in his driveway when Gordo arrived midafternoon. I watched them talking out the window. Gordo walked gingerly down our path and came inside, "Dave generously offered to lend us one of his cars until we figure out a plan," he said.

"That's great. Do you want to lie down?" I asked.

"No, going to take a bunch of Advil and then I'd really like to leave the house. Do something fun. Uplifting." Gordo poured himself a glass of water. "Hey, why don't we go see the new Marvel movie?" he asked.

"Of course," I replied. After dinner that night, we headed out to power-eat popcorn and watch superheroes kick ass. On the way there, Luke and I got a ping from Power School. I turned my head to look at him in the backseat.

"You are kidding me Luke– 2 F's" I said.

"I have to get gas," Gordo announced, "Should I do it now or after the movies?" he asked.

"Are you tone deaf," I snapped. I'd been navigating the kids' issues completely solo, and it was wearing me down.

"Dad, who cares? Just get the gas." Luke said.

Gordo pulled into the Sunoco station. *Sorry he whispered* before getting out. The moment his door shut; Luke burst into tears. "You have no idea what's going on in my life," he stammered, "It's a miracle I only have 2 F's."

My anger evaporated instantly. I unclicked my seatbelt and turned around. "I can't know if you don't tell me," I said lovingly. What is going on?" I looked into his eyes. They shivered with fear. Then the floodgates opened, and it all came out.

"Last week I was locked in the bathroom and forced to vape. They said it was my *initiation*. The same kids invited me out last weekend. I don't know why I went. I wished I hadn't. They got me high and then two pick-up trucks pulled up. The guys got out with shotguns and said we were on their property and to get off. They started coming after us. We ran. I got separated. Didn't know where I was, so I hid in the bushes for over an hour until I thought they'd gone and then walked three miles home across Embarcadero using my phone for GPS," he said tears streaming down his face. His body was shaking. I put my hand on his knee. There was no next move. No way forward here.

Gordo got back in the car. Luke brushed away the tears, "Let's go," he said. "I will raise my grades. I'm sorry." Gordo looked at me. I shook my head *not right now*.

We arrived at the theatre, waited online for popcorn. Luke turned toward me, whispered in my ear "Those are the dudes from the other night," he said gesturing to two guys in hoodies near the entrance.

"Luke and I are going to save our seats," I said. I put my arm around him, walking behind the concession stand out of view. We found our row. Sat down. "I am so sorry Luke. We are going to figure this out," I said.

He held my hand, "I'm sorry I didn't tell you." I clenched my jaw so I wouldn't cry, "That is on me. I should have seen it. Should have noticed. I wanted to believe this would all work out. I am sorrier than I could ever tell you," I said.

Finley and Gordo arrived with buckets of popcorn, sodas, and Bunch-a Crunch. I relayed the story to Gordo over previews. Cried for the first half of the movie. Stared blankly at the empty seat in front of me for the second. Afterwards, we walked back to the car in silence. Pulled out of the parking lot. "Gordo, stop the car," I said sternly. I turned around. Looked at Luke, "We are going home. Home, home," I said.

"You mean Connecticut?" Finley asked.

"Yes," I said still staring at Luke "This is the end. There is no new strategy. We are leaving. That is a promise. Daddy and I will figure out the details," I said.

"Really," Luke asked hopefully. Then concerned he added, "I don't want to ruin this for dad." Tears fell down Gordo's cheeks.

He looked back at Luke, "Buddy, you could never ruin anything. You mean the world to me. I'm so sorry I haven't been present. This job has clouded my judgment, but it is crystal clear now. We are leaving." Six months after arriving, without ever truly landing, we plotted our exit.

Confronting the King of Spam and a Red-Headed Troll

Gordo planned to promote *Altitude,* the Canna Bliss line of beverages with a splashy launch in Lake Tahoe to kick off ski season. He'd secured the sponsorship months earlier. We planned a family vacation around it. He'd have to work a lot, but the boys could snowboard. I'd explore the area and we could meet up for meals. It would be a blast. That weekend was now one week away. Several days before we left, Gordo received a PIP from Dirk. We'd never heard of a PIP before. It sounded like it should come with striped stockings and candy canes. Gordo's particular *Performance Improvement Plan* was a CYA character assassination issued after he refused to advertise the five million surplus cartons of E-Juice Vapes that had been linked to bubble lung in the press.

"You need to lawyer up immediately," his friend Clark told him in the parking lot. No one spoke openly in the office. Dirk had microphones planted everywhere.

Gordo thought it seemed extreme, so he called Dave on the way home. Told him the whole story. "People go to jail for this kind of thing," Dave said, "Whatever you do, do NOT sign the PIP. Your consent is tantamount to admitting that everything they've accused you of is true. They're framing you as the scapegoat in case this whole thing goes sideways. It's reprehensible that they'd release that product. I'm proud of you for standing up," Dave said.

Strange thing to say to another grown man. It seemed like a rather obvious decision, but Dave's sincerity made Gordo a little nervous. "What else would I do. It's a public health threat," Gordo responded.

"You'd be surprised," Dave replied, "It's a high-pressure situation. People cave. Especially when they have a family."

Gordo fell silent. "Not to be naïve but how do you go to jail for something you stood up against," Gordo said.

"Happens out here all the time. Don't worry. I know a shrewd corporate attorney. He owes me. Plus, he'll do this on principal alone."

Before Gordo got home Dave had made the introduction to Blake, a cut-throat lawyer originally from Missouri who'd retired to Napa Valley with his wife. Gordo called him immediately and put him on speaker so I could hear the gameplan.

He had a southern drawl and laser focus. "We are going to take our time," he told Gordo, "They're setting up to fire you. Probably incriminate you for things you didn't do. We're not going to let that happen. I need you to create a diary from the day you started. Be as detailed as you can. Everything is going to be right as rain. You go to Lake Tahoe with your family. Have a good time. Don't sign that PIP. I'm going to do some poking around. By the time you get back we will have a retort that makes this Silicon Valley troll think twice about messing with you," Blake said. He was a chess player. You could feel it in his composure. Calm, unhurried, calculating. Dirk would have no idea what was coming.

The house had been pre-paid so despite manufacturing delays and violent threats from Dirk, we piled the dogs and boys into a rented Explorer and took off. The official kick-off would be delayed but Gordo had meetings to pave the way for local distribution. Low-grade tension followed us but there was a ray of hope. We rode it straight to Squaw Valley. The boys were excited.

Us too. We'd never been skiing in California. November was early, but Gordo confirmed they were open. As we got close, the mountain looked brownish green.

Luke looked up from his phone, "Dad, where's the snow?" he asked.

"Maybe there was a warm snap," I said nervously, "Let's pull in and ask." Gordo turned into the nearly empty Tahoe Mountain parking lot and went inside.

He returned smiling. "Good news. The bunny hill is open and– one blue run. They said we'd probably want to ski in the morning as is gets a bit wet by afternoon." Not ideal but doable. We arrived at the house. Seven bedrooms. Ten-person hot tub. Two-story great room fireplace. Triple-mint kitchen. Full game room.

"Pick whatever room you want. Maybe a different one each night," I said. The boys scattered. The house was spectacular. But more than all the amenities, it felt like a solid home base– the perfect place to face the minefield of challenges ahead of us. That night, Gordo stayed up till the wee hours creating a diary that documented every nefarious, discriminatory, book-cooking, embezzling act of white-collar crime he'd witnessed per Blake's request.

The next morning, we got to work. Every decision felt like it had an *or else* on the back end. We needed to get out of our obscenely expensive California lease *or else* we'd have to rob a bank. We needed to break the lease with our Connecticut renters *or else* we'd be stuck finding a seven-month rental with two dogs in January. I called our landlord, Shinya, that afternoon and explained our situation from Luke's depression to Gordo's inevitable job loss and potential jail threat. I asked if she'd be willing to release us from the lease. "I know you will probably need to keep the security deposit," I said, "We will keep the house show ready and I will find someone to sublet…"

She interrupted me, "Don't worry. I will handle it. This happens all the time out here. Take care of your family. Please tell Gordo this is not his fault. People who fail at their first endeavor are twice as likely to succeed at the next. Chin up. You will get through this," she said. I was braced for the worst. Her kindness stunned me.

Maybe I'd misunderstood. Maybe she meant we could leave but she'd have to keep our two-month security. "So, should we…" I stammered not sure how to ask directly without appearing ungrateful.

"I am releasing you from the lease," she clarified as if reading my mind. "Let me know what day you want to end it. I will refund your full security as long there's no damage." My shoulders softened. Face relaxed. Grace flooded my body. "Thank you," I replied. "Be strong," she said. We hung up. We had a long way to go but the universe felt aligned.

Having cut short our California lease, we'd need to kick it into high gear to get back into our real house early. Gordo had a call the next morning with our renter back East. Terrence was the CEO of a data company. His family's primary residence was a five-million-dollar penthouse on Park Avenue. Gordo had spoken with his assistant. She said they planned to use our house on weekends but had only been a couple times. Given the circumstances, she couldn't imagine it would be a problem. Feeling confident about our future, we left to buy groceries at Tahoe Central Market. We drank fresh-squeezed orange juice samples, sang with the cheesy yacht rock songs, and got food for the week.

The next day Gordo left early with the boys to snowboard. His call with Terrence was at 11:00. He found an empty room at the lodge and got ready. It was a vulnerable conversation to have with a total stranger. But his assistant had been encouraging so Gordo was hopeful. Terrence was forty-five minutes late. When Gordo finally reached him, he shared our situation, offering a month free rent and guaranteed security deposit back. Terrence paused before replying. "I pride myself on being an empathetic person and creative-problem-solver, but I'm going to have to go with a hard no."

Gordo was dumbfounded. "Your assistant said you are only using it as an occasional getaway," he said.

"That's right," Terrence replied, "It was hard to find a place and we really like your house, so we are going to stay. Got to run. Good luck," he said.

Gordo called me flabbergasted, "Not going to happen," he said, "He actually told me it was a *hard no*," he added.

"Are you kidding," I replied, "He wouldn't even consider it?" I asked.

"Nope. I looked back at our ring doorbell footage to see if they'd move anything in. Nothing. Just he and his two obese teenagers walking their dog with miner hats at night. Then leaving in their gold Tesla with an *I heart SPAM* bumper sticker."

I sat down, flooded with defeat. "What a douchebag," I said.

"I looked him up," Gordo continued, "Apparently, the *data* company he runs is more of a junk mail operation. Largest in North America. We are renting to the King of Spam." We sat in silence. "The boys have been waiting," Gordo said, "I've got to meet them for lunch." We hung up.

I reached out to our Connecticut neighbor, Nathalie, who'd been keeping an eye on things while we were gone. *They won't let us back in our house,* I texted. She replied, *What a-holes… They've closed every blind and shutter so I can't see in. I'm sure your realtor told you, but they were on an episode of Hoarders.* My eyes nearly popped out of my head. I clicked on the link. There they were– for real. Um, no, our realtor had failed to cross-check that. *Ugh,* I responded. *Please, keep me updated.* Luckily, our contract stipulated that our housekeeper cleaned once a week so at least we had someone on the inside.

Since Terrence refused to leave our house, it was a full-fledged fire drill to find a seven-month rental that took dogs. It would need to be furnished as we had no budget for moving expenses. Plus, we'd be back in our real home soon enough. I scrolled through options. The most promising one had a stained Laura Ashley couch, futon beds, and cracked Formica counters. I closed my laptop and stared out at the pine trees. Some had a dusting of snow. Mostly bare branches. Beautiful but austere. A minute later, my phone buzzed– a text from my sister Tina. *We want you home safe and sound. It is a gift. No need to pay it back.*

I called Gordo. "What is happening," I asked.

"They just wired forty thousand dollars into our account," he said. I was speechless. "Kels, I don't know what to say. They've been my rock out here. I talk to them almost every day." Gordo's voice faltered, "This job has been impossible, and I was so worried about you and Luke. And now…" he tried to steady his voice, "I didn't want to tell you, but Dirk is threatening to fire me and sue us for the entire relocation package. I'm so sorry," he said. I closed my eyes. Tried to process my gratitude, rage, and relief.

"It's okay," I replied, "You've relayed this all to Blake, right?" I asked.

"Of course," he said. We had a lot to do.

"Let's assume it will all work out," I added. There wasn't time to evaluate if-then scenarios. "I'm going to expand our rental search to unfurnished. Enjoy those last mud, oops, I mean ski runs," I said joking.

That night, we checked To Do boxes in front of roaring fires. I filled out the roughly ten thousand forms to get the boys out of Palo Alto schools and back into Westport. Gordo talked strategy with Blake. We discussed worst-case work scenarios over cinnamon spice tea while the boys hot tubbed. Finley came in wearing one of the oversized complimentary bathrobes. He stretched out on the couch and wrapped himself in fur blankets. "Can I get you anything," Gordo teased.

"My phone would be nice," Finley said half-kidding. Gordo handed it to him. Luke texted his lacrosse coaches he'd be home for spring season. They responded immediately. He smiled and showed us their message: *Welcome back buddy! You're on*

Varsity. No try-out necessary. Can't wait to have you on the team. Ordering your helmet right now.

We made big family breakfasts and tried to keep the mood light but after Dirk's twentieth text threatening to fire Gordo if he didn't return, we left a day early. I drove. Gordo tried to coordinate moving companies and airlines for over an hour. "The only movers available in December need to pick up on the 24th and the only flights available to travel with dogs isn't until the 29th, he said.

"We'll figure it out," I replied, "I'll call Gabby and Lisa—try to piece together the last five nights. Can you call the vet. Make sure the dogs have whatever shots they need to travel," I said.

"Yup," Gordo responded, "and I'm going to list your car on eBay, so we don't have to pay for transport. With the damage from getting rear-ended at Trader Joe's, it isn't worth it. We can figure out new cars when we get home." The boys slept. We weren't out of the woods yet, but we were a few steps closer.

Hunting for Houses and a White-Collar Criminal

By the time we got back to Palo Alto, Blake had emailed his retort. It was riveting– riddled with scathing criminal implications. Not only did it refute every accusation they'd made; it outlined back-up evidence to the contrary. Detailed the highly abusive work conditions. Called Dirk out for regularly threatening bodily harm. The rebuttal concluded with an off-hand addendum that outlined clear-cut documented examples of corporate embezzlement, tax fraud and public health endangerment for sale of knowingly tainted products. The very last sentence assured management that Gordo had no *current* intention of releasing any of this information to officials or the investors about to release the last twenty-million-dollar tranche. I read it in disbelief.

"Wow," I said, "Is this all true?"

Gordo nodded. "Every bit of it. You know that cannabis trade show we attended? The booth that should have cost twenty to thirty thousand. The tab was two hundred and fifty thousand dollars. No itemized list. Just one lump sum payable to a company that had no website. I took it to Jim in finance. He traced it back to one of the board members. Jim brought it to Dirk's attention and was fired two hours later. I was told to keep my mouth shut." I set the retort on the kitchen counter.

"That is scandalous. Why didn't you tell me any of this?" I asked.

"You had your hands full trying to keep our real life from going off the rails. You know Steve, the CMO before me that we were told had a nervous breakdown? Our IT guy Marc showed me emails Dirk mistakenly sent to him, thinking it was the *CCO,*

Steve. They read: *I can't bring Steven. We don't need a fag fucking up the meeting.*"

My eyes turned to saucers. "This is crazy," I replied.

"It goes on and on," Gordo continued, "It's the most messed up culture I've ever been a part of it. Besides being totally corrupt, they're completely paranoid. Blake told me to copy files in case we need them for evidence, but every computer is locked, so Marc had to set up an invisible FTP site for me to download all Dirk's emails.

Gordo called Blake to thank him for the retort. "Oh, my dear boy," Blake said, "We are just beginning. It is going to get very ugly. They are not going to be happy about this. I am guessing given their tone you have been compliant until now," he said.

"I have," Gordo replied.

Blake continued, "So, this is going to come as a bit of a shock. You aren't going to mention a word about me. You wrote this– they will know you have counsel but no need to poke the bear any more yet. They will make all kinds of threats. Just smile and keep going to work. This is a long game. Hand a hard copy to Dirk. Email him and every board member as well right after. Do it all at the end of the day. Will make dinner time more fun for them. Leave directly after." Gordo did as he was directed.

Before getting even a mile away from the office that night, his phone blew up with texts. *Dude, what did you do? Dirk is on a rampage. He just locked chief counsel in a conference room and is screaming at the top of his lungs.* For the first time since we'd arrived, Gordo turned off his phone for dinner. We took the boys to Mayfield Bakery and Café. Got ice cream after. Stopped at 18-8 Fine Men's Salons to get them impromptu haircuts for our Thanksgiving trip home. Gordo and I meandered around while we waited. Perused the bookstore with a calm we hadn't felt in months. Gordo had been through hell, but his spirit was returning. I felt grateful. There was no telling where it would all end up. But we were in good hands with Blake.

Work blew up into a full-scale tornado. Dirk threatened lawsuits daily. Told Gordo he knew the Sheriff and would have him arrested. Accused him of crimes he hadn't committed. "Stay calm. Just do your job and go home," Blake kept telling him. Gordo was nervous for us to take our Thanksgiving trip. "Take it," Blake said, "Plus, you are going to put in for vacation time over the last week in December now, so they'll be obligated to pay you whether he fires you or you quit. Your employment contract covers that. Might as well make sure you get it," Blake added calmly.

"Dirk is going to flip out. Have a coronary," Gordo said.

"Well now that would make thing easier, wouldn't it," Blake replied. "No one at work can know your endgame. We're playing chess here. Every move counts. And right now, they have no idea we even have a master plan. Just keep doing a great job. We will keep responding to things as they come. If they fire you, we will negotiate your package. If not, Christmas Eve you will quit," Blake said.

"Sounds so matter of fact when you say it," Gordo said.

"It is," Blake responded. Gordo put in for Christmas vacation. Dirk went through the roof. Threatened everything but assassination. The next day we flew east for Thanksgiving.

The house-hunting schedule was aggressive. We needed to have a rental locked and loaded before we left. First, we met up with friends for a home-coming holiday lunch. It felt like an eternity since we'd said good-bye four months ago. The long table was filled with wine, salads and laughter, beer, burgers, and stories. We hugged goodbye knowing we'd see each other soon. Soon did not feel soon enough. What we had to fit into the next four weeks felt gargantuan. That afternoon we met our realtor at the end of a dark dead-end road across from the highway. "Nope," I said.

"This is one of the ones you sent," she replied.

"Internet photos showed a different picture," I responded. We didn't go in. The second house was a one-story ranch with a white marble foyer across from a scrubby back lawn. "Possible," I said dubiously. We took the full tour.

"They said they'd get rid of the bathroom mildew and the mouse traps are old," our realtor relayed.

"I think we will pass but thank you," I said. The last house was closer to the schools. It had a couple broken blinds, a creepy basement, and a bunch of dead stinkbugs but high ceilings and lots of windows. Sold. We negotiated on the spot. Signed the next day.

"Do you want to drive by our old house on the way back to your sister's?" Gordo asked.

"Sure," I replied, not at all sure I did. Every blind was pulled. The driveway was littered with *New York Times* papers. Groceries sat outside the front door. "Not doing that again," I said.

Thanksgiving was bittersweet. My sister Tina always hosted. She and Rob put out a spectacular spread. Between bites of cranberry-smothered turkey I kept thinking about how grateful we were to be coming back to Connecticut. I just wished it was to our real home. Tina pulled me aside after dinner. "Gordo said you guys have three nights when you get back before you get into your rental. Stay here. Use the cars. We are away but the house is all yours," she said.

"That is huge, thank you," I replied. We had a west coast whirlwind awaiting us. I still had to figure out where we'd sleep for the five nights between the movers coming and our flight home.

When we got back to Palo Alto, I invited Gabby for tea to tell her our news and ask if we could stay in one of their homes for that interim period. "Thanks so much for coming over," I said.

"Oh my gosh, it's so great to see you," she replied giving me a big hug. "I'm sorry I've been so absent. I know you've tried to get us together. John and I have been traveling a lot and we just started construction on his study addition," she said.

"Don't be silly," I responded, "I know you guys are busy. Scone?" I offered holding up a plate, "They're ginger. Made them this morning."

Gabby held up a dark green bottle of liquid. "Doing this silly cleanse but they look delicious," she replied. "How are you all holding up?" she asked. "Is there anything I can do? Do the boys want to come for a swim?" she offered. It was kind, we needed more than a swim.

"I'm sure they'd love to," I replied, "But there is something kind of important I wanted to ask you."

Gabby leaned in. "Of course," she said her smile becoming more serious.

"We have to be out of this house on the 24th but there were no flights with dogs until the 29th, so I was hoping maybe if your cottage is free or one of your other homes." I added hopefully.

"Oh no," she said sadly, "I'm so sorry but I have a friend going through chemotherapy who is staying in the guest house. It's a tragic story," she said. "The kids are at the Carmel Valley house for the holiday and John's surfing buddy is in our Malibu place, but..." she added starting to get excited, "The condo in Laguna Beach might be possible and it's right down the beach from the house we just finished building. So, you and the boys will have to come for dinner," she concluded.

"That would be amazing," I replied.

Then looking at Floyd and Zezu sleeping she scrunched her face into an apology. "Except John is kind of particular– I don't think he'll be okay with the dogs." she said. "Can you board them?" she asked.

"Um, no, not really," I replied. "They didn't do well on the flight here and I don't want to leave them for four days before we do it again." I took a sip of my tea. Tried to swallow my disappointment. "I guess we'll figure something else out," I said.

"I will definitely ask him and let you know," she added, putting her hand on my knee. "I'm just so happy you can finally go home. I know how hard this has been for you." She didn't know the half of it.

"Just a few bumps in the road. All good," I said not up for sympathy.

She sat back. "I never really pictured you out here. I had that feeling before you even came. Strange, right?" I wasn't sure how to respond. "But you are going home. That's all that matters now," she added.

"Absolutely," I replied. We chatted a bit longer. I couldn't shake my frustration. They were not my houses. I had no right to feel resentful. We stood up to say goodbye,

"You seem upset," she said.

"No, no," I said setting my tea on the counter. "Just stressed about getting everything done in a short time." We hugged.

"Let me know if you need anything," she said. I smiled. "Well, anything *else*," she added. I watched her blond bob walk down our front path.

Serving Pomegranate Martinis and Pancakes

We had two weeks to pack the house, dodge a lawsuit, host two holiday parties and prepare for a house full of boys. Not to mention we still needed to figure out where we'd stay for the four days between the movers and our flight. We looked at dog-friendly hotels, but our stay fell over Christmas, so they were either astronomically expensive or fully booked. We are not a big camping family but pitching a tent was looking like a strong possibility. Meantime, we had two holiday parties to host.

The first was for Gordo's all-star colleagues. They'd been incredibly supportive during a difficult time. They too had given up great jobs. Moved their families far distances only to become hostages handcuffed by contracts. Gordo was deeply grateful. We wanted to say thank you, but he wouldn't be resigning until the day before we left so there could be NO visible signs we were moving. No evidence of packing boxes. The charade had to be pitch-perfect. The second party was to say goodbye to all the friends who'd been so kind and generous. We'd leave behind nothing but gratitude.

The house needed to look festive, so we made a late-night trip to Home Goods. Picked up five hundred feet of glittery cranberry balls and fake pine tree branches. Strung the house with cheap joy. Bought top-shelf booze and created a signature pomegranate martini. I went into hostess mode for two nights. Both parties went off flawlessly. Gabby called the day after, "What a wonderful party. I'm sorry it took so long but John said you are welcome to stay at our condo in Laguna. The dogs must stay in the downstairs room," she said.

"Thank you so much. That takes a ton of pressure off. We really appreciate it," I replied.

"I will email you directions about how to get into the house and fun things to do. We will be down there the last night, so we'd love to have you all for dinner," she added.

"That would be wonderful," I said. The next couple days, we packed like overcaffeinated worker bees.

The only way we'd gotten Luke off *Fortnite* and out of his bedroom our second month there was by promising he could have all his friends visit before Christmas break. Luke's buddies would be arriving in two days and departing the day before our movers came. We considered cancelling, but they had non-refundable tickets. Plus, it would be the memory of a lifetime. So, a couple days after the parties, Gordo and Luke picked up his five best friends at SFO airport. Two hours later, boisterous boy energy swung through our back door. The entry was littered with sneakers. Gordo looked at me. "Nothing better," he said.

"The best," I replied. The house was small for seven boys, but they filled it with joy. Emptied it of food. Slept on couches. They snuck onto Stanford Fields for a football catch and played ping-pong downtown. Gordo got box seats to a Sharks game. I flipped what seemed like ten thousand pancakes in the morning and eavesdropped on their conversation.

"Dude, why would you ever leave here," his friend Jack said.

"Yeah man, you are living the California dream," Ollie added. Three days flew by in fun-filled flurry. Thursday morning, the boys packed up and we headed to the airport. I took them through security to the gate and hugged them goodbye. I had a mountain of packing still in front me. As I was leaving, the flight attendant called me over. "You can't leave the boys unattended. You need to wait until they've boarded the plane," she said.

She must be kidding. The flight was not for another two hours. The movers would be at our house in twenty-four. I considered protesting but her expression suggested that might not be a good idea. So, I opted to buy the new *Oprah*, devour chocolate-covered almonds, and check on Gordo to make sure he and Finley weren't watching cartoons eating Lucky Charms waiting for me to return. An eternity passed. Finally, I got home. We stuffed boxes late into the night. Gordo had a meeting scheduled with Dirk the next morning.

"He seriously doesn't suspect anything?" I asked.

"Are you kidding. He sees it as another opportunity to reprimand me. He is going to be dumbfounded," Gordo replied taping up the last box before bed.

"You're not going to torch the place to the ground, right?" I asked, "Because I know you'd like to."

Gordo put his arm around me. "I have it all planned out. I'm not looking to preserve anything here. It's over and I finally have an opportunity to speak my mind. But I won't do anything stupid," he promised.

"You've talked to Blake about every inch of what you're going to say, right?" I confirmed.

"Of course," Gordo replied. "The resignation letter he wrote is brilliant. I will tender it tomorrow, but it doesn't take effect until the end of our vacation two weeks from now.

I smiled. "Turnabout is sweet justice," I said.

"Dirk is going to lose his shit," Gordo said reveling in the firework finale he'd meticulously planned.

"Just please be careful," I begged, "Don't say anything that can be used against us later." I taped up the last box. We brushed our teeth and went to bed. Slept like babies.

The next morning, I got up and made coffee. Gordo's meeting with Dirk was at 8am. "Have a great day at the office," I said giving him good luck kiss.

"Oh, it will be," Gordo replied and off he went.

I vacuumed every room and scrubbed every toilet. I wanted Shinya to know how much we appreciated her kindness. At 9:40 I still hadn't heard form Gordo. The movers would be at the house in a couple hours. I called him.

"I'm so sorry, I am almost home. Was going to call you but as you can imagine it was a little crazy. Dirk went on a rampage. I got calls from every exec team member wanting to hear what happened," he said.

"Did you send your resignation to the board before they turned off your email?" I asked.

"Yup. They still haven't turned it off," he replied.

"What did you say to Dirk?" I asked cringing at the possibilities.

"I told him I wanted to speak about one word. Perspective. That from where he sat, he thought he was in control. But from my side of the desk, he had nothing but hubris and a job that was crumbling as we spoke. I was resigning but eventually he'd lose everything. I told him I didn't like him. Nobody did. That if I saw him coming down the hall on my way to the bathroom, I'd go around the entire building just to avoid him."

I sat down on one of the moving boxes. "You said *all* that?" I asked.

"Sure did," Gordo replied. "I also told him that in my thirties I would have tried to please him. In my forties I would have tried to take his job. But at fifty I was just going to leave him to his own demise," Gordo said.

"What did he say back?" I asked.

"He turned red, then purple, then shouted at me to get out of his office. *Good luck*, I told him and left. Myrtle asked when I'd be back. *Not in this life,* I told her. I walked out, got into the Suburban, and pulled out of that crappy parking lot for the last time. And, you are going to love this, for the first time since I started this job, I did not get lost coming home."

Part Four:
Surviving a Tsunami

Torching the Job Before the Big Getaway

I knew moving cross-country with a litigious psycho on our heels would not be a cakewalk. Dirk would soon erupt into a tidal wave of terror. But we'd survived California. We'd surf whatever tsunami he sent our way. Gordo got back to the house. The day shifted into warp speed. Movers packed our belongings. Bizarre to think we'd be seeing all our California furniture back east in a couple of weeks. I checked the house one last time to make sure we hadn't left anything. Totally empty save for the orchid, bottle of wine and heartfelt note we'd left for Shinya on the kitchen counter. A clean slate for someone new. Dave and Lisa had offered to host a goodbye dinner for us. So, that evening, we walked across Washington Street– California conquistadors.

Lisa taught Finley how to wash pomegranate seeds. Luke and I chopped veggies for the salad. Dave and Gordo talked about Canna Bliss. "They are not all like that you know," Dave said. "If you guys wanted to stay, I could definitely make some introductions." He swirled his scotch as if stirring up new possibilities.

"That is super generous," Gordo replied, "But this move is about Luke. We need to get him home. Who knows, I may be back," he added. They both knew he wouldn't. "You and Lisa have been rocks for us here. I can't thank you enough. Truly, man, I don't know what we would have done without you," Gordo said.

"We've loved having you here," Dave replied.

"I can't believe you are leaving tomorrow," Lisa said sadly, handing me a salad bowl for our veggies.

"Me neither," I said. My nerves were too keyed up for reflection. We ate dinner and watched *Star Wars: Return of the Jedi* together. They'd offered to let us spend the night, so we didn't have to drive to Laguna in the dark. We went to bed in their state-of-the-art basement. The next morning, Gordo and I woke up early. Drank coffee. Walked the dogs. Got ready to depart. Lisa made to-go bagels for the boys, and they escorted us to the car.

As I hugged her goodbye, it hit me. This chapter was over. Really over. We'd no longer be meeting for coffee in the middle of the street. Friendships built on proximity often fade. The finality of it took my breath away. We loved them in a way they'd never fully understand– like firemen that save you from a burning building. Too big to say. Too big not to. I turned around before opening my car door. Looked back at Lisa. Held my hand to my heart. Mouthed thank you. Then, we piled into the Suburban and drove down the Oregon Expressway to the 101 for the last time. It was a strange feeling– like we had both cheated death and yet failed to stay long enough.

Laguna Beach was an eight-hour drive. We stopped at gas stations for snacks and a UPS store to ship the dog beds we'd forgotten to give the movers. Gordo asked about the slowest, least expensive option. "Isn't there something for less if we genuinely don't need it for months," Gordo asked the guy.

"Even if you send it by horse and carriage, it's going be over one thousand dollars per bed," the guy said. We left with our oversized dog beds in hand. No idea what we'd do with them.

After the last Sunoco stop for Doritos, gummy-bears, and Arizona iced teas, I checked the GPS– two and half hours, "Okay boys we're in the home stretch. Christmas Eve tonight in Laguna Beach," I announced.

"It's going to be weird not being with Aunt Tina and everyone," Luke said.

"Yeah, with no Christmas tree or snow," Finley added.

"True, but we *are* one step closer to home. You guys decide whatever you want for dinner," I said.

"Captain Crunch?" Finley asked.

"Sure," I said,

"*That's* what you want on Christmas Eve," Luke commented sarcastically.

"Why not," Finley joked, "maybe with eggnog instead of milk," he added for fun.

"We're not having cereal for Christmas Eve dinner," Luke replied. They debated back and forth. Ultimately, we decided to see what inspired us at the grocery store once we arrived. A few hours later we pulled into the driveway of Gabby's condo in Laguna. The boys walked the dogs. Gordo got the key from under the potted plant. I began unloading bags. We were flat-out exhausted, so I made Keurig coffee. As I turned to hand Gordo his cup, my foot caught on the edge of the dining room table, and coffee spilled all over the white linen chair cover.

"Oh my god you are kidding me," I said, "I am an idiot. I guess I should be staying in the basement too." Frantic, I stripped off the slipcover, ran to the sink, washed it with cold water and soap but the brown stain was still there. Faded but not gone. "Gordo please check if they have Spray n' Wash," I said. They did. He pre-cleaned it and threw it in the washing machine. I collapsed in a heap on the floor. I couldn't take disappointing anyone else or feeling more like a failure. The fate of Christmas and my mental well-being were on spin cycle. Luckily for everyone, it came clean.

Dumping Dog Beds at Midnight in Laguna Beach

Grocery shopping is where our family really shines. It is somehow exempt from the normal *go at a million miles an hour until you crash into a wall* approach. We got a cart and entered Ralph's– the swankiest supermarket on the West Coast. Usually, it's filled with colorful characters, but it being Christmas Eve, there were almost no customers. The boys disappeared. Gordo and I browsed the premade tea aisle. The Fugees, *Killing Me Softly* came on over the loudspeakers. I spun around, grabbed my imaginary microphone, and sung to Gordo, "*Strumming my pain with his fingers...*" He pretended not to notice me. Examined a box of peach teabags. I continued- holding my arm out dramatically, "*Singing my life with his word ...*" He looked around me nonchalantly– pretending to study tea options. I threw up two fingers in front of the Green Matcha. Belted out "*Two times two times.*" He smiled, "Okay, okay," he said throwing a box of ginger tea into the cart.

At the far end of the aisle a boy whizzed by in a motorized shopping cart. His legs were crossed. He held a finger to his cheek in thinker pose. Gordo burst out laughing. I didn't have my glasses on. "Was that Finley?" I asked.

"Yup. That's your son," Gordo said. We watched the end of the aisle hoping for an encore. A minute later, he came back the other way, this time reclined with his hands clasped behind his head and Luke chasing him from behind. He stopped mid-aisle, put Luke in the basket, and they drove off. Next time we saw them they were drag-racing their motorized shopping carts through the produce section. We stocked the cart with Finley's favorite

Japanese marble soda pop, orange Gatorade for Luke, fajitas for Christmas Eve dinner and staples for the week.

Christmas morning, I made blueberry muffins and hot chocolate for the boys. "I put the presents Aunt Tina and Uncle Rob sent on the dining room table," I said, "I'm sorry Santa is a little light this year– but Mrs. Claus did find a great breakfast place in town that's open. We can go when I get back from my run," I said. We watched them open presents. Then I laced up my running shoes and ran south along the ocean. Running slows down my mind. The Pacific spread out before me. Long stretch of beach as far as the eye could see. Beautiful, but it wasn't home. I'm partial to the dark blue Atlantic with its craggy coastline, mystery tucked into every crevice.

Christmas brunch was amazing. Fresh squeezed grapefruit juice. Organic farm eggs. Hearty servings of buttermilk pancakes and Canadian bacon. Over the next few days, the boys and I shopped, cooked, and played on the beach. Gordo talked nonstop to Dirk's executive director, Lilah. She said they might be willing to overlook his gross dereliction of duties but there was no way Gordo wouldn't get out of reimbursing them for the full relocation package. Gordo told her he had no intention of sharing the ghost drive he'd copied with Dirk's direction to release the tainted product or his prejudicial harassment of the last CMO, but they would need to pay three months' severance. The game of cat and mouse escalated and then went silent. Christmas dinner had decidedly less ho, ho, ho than years past.

Our last night, Gabby and John invited us all for dinner. The house they'd built was literally a short walk down the beach.

We ate sushi together on the beautiful balsam table John had made in his workshop. After dinner, he gave us a tour that culminated on the roof deck with a glass of wine. There was a full bar and sunken hot tub. Every detail was executed for ultimate elegance and maximum views. We looked out at the sunset. Spectacular orange sky. Sparkling water. Moon rising in the distance. A magical West Coast night. We soaked it all in, thanked them for a beautiful time and walked back to their condo holding hands. "One last swim?" Gordo asked. Finley stripped off his shirt. Ditched his flip-flops off and dove in. Gordo and Luke right behind him. I watched, smiling. Our dystopian adventure had a fairytale ending.

That night we did a full-house check to make sure we hadn't forgotten anything. The large dog beds glared back at me from the entryway. "Shit, Gordo, what are we going to do with these?" I asked.

"Maybe we leave them as a parting gift for Gabby," he said half-joking.

"I'm sure they'd love that. Seriously," I replied.

"Yeah, I have no idea," Gordo responded unhelpfully.

"Well, we need to figure it out," I said impatiently, "Boys put the beds in the back of the Suburban. We are going to have to dump them somewhere."

Gordo laughed "Like on a street corner," he said sarcastically.

"Well, do you have a better idea?" I asked. I dragged one of them through the front door to the Suburban.

"Oh my god, you're serious," Gordo said, "Kels, dumping is illegal you know. There are store and street cameras everywhere."

I hoisted it up and threw it in the far back. "Okay," I said, "Why don't we just bring them to the airport tomorrow and see how much *they* will charge. Is that a good idea?"

Gordo got the other dog bed and put in the back, "Boys– let's go. We are going to try not to get arrested before our flight tomorrow morning," he said.

We left the complex at ten o'clock. Drove around Laguna looking for back alleys with big dumpsters. Laughed till our bellies hurt at the absurdity. "I know," I said triumphantly after we'd trolled every strip mall on the outskirts of town, "We will leave them in front of a dog shelter with a note saying it is a donation." The car was quiet for a minute.

"That's actually not a bad idea Mom," Luke said. I looked up shelters.

"YES! I declared, "Five miles away." Finley wrote the note. We dumped our donation. The next morning was a blur. We executed the emotional dog drop-off with fewer tears knowing we would all be where we belonged soon. Dropped the Suburban. Made our flight.

Profanity, Stinkbugs and Personal Metamorphosis

We arrived at JFK. Cops hollering, "Let's go! let's go!" Cabbies honking, "Get out of my fuckin' way." Bronx accents with brass balls sucking back cigarettes from the curb. It smelled like freedom. Sounded like home. Something about New York grit grounds me. It hadn't changed. But we had. I felt like Odysseus returning to Ithaca. Familiar yet strange. Our family dynamic was different. We were closer; yet more independent. Broken; yet more resilient. We didn't talk about it, but the silence was filled with it. One by one we pulled our bags off the scrolling carousel and waited outside for Julio. How would we each re-enter our old lives with our new selves?

Luke's maturity had cost his innocence. He was returning as a young man to his boyhood friends. Some experiences can't be explained. Not to mention they'd have new inside jokes and stories he hadn't been a part of. Their visit to California had existed in a bubble. Now that we were back, he'd have to navigate caterpillar terrain from a butterfly perspective without abandoning whom he'd become. Heavy lifting for a fifteen-year-old. Finley was different too. Freedom had changed him. He'd biked everywhere. Drank Bobo. Surfed new horizons. Tasted a California we hadn't. Developed an appetite for adventure that would have to find a new translation. Gordo was returning from California as a KPI-crushing, capital raising, tech-savvy dynamo but none of it would matter if he couldn't recover his confidence.

"Julio texted. They wouldn't let him park, so he had to circle back around. Said it would be about ten minutes," Gordo relayed.

"I don't care *how* long it takes. We are HOME! Conquering heroes with a bold adventure under our belts," I exclaimed.

Gordo laughed. "*Conquering heroes* might be a stretch. Pretty sure that requires having *conquered* something," he said jokingly. He moved the boys' luggage closer to ours. "Or at least not failing at what you set out to do," he added. His tone was light-hearted, but he wasn't kidding.

"I don't know," I said, "I think escaping an abusive situation and refusing to commit crimes endangering peoples' lives qualifies as heroic."

We'd had this discussion before. It didn't matter that in Silicon Valley, failing was as ordinary and essential as oxygen. Dave had failed at a bunch of start-ups. Congratulated Gordo on his first. Called it a rite of passage. The question wasn't *why* but *what next*. Unfortunately, Gordo saw it differently. Being professionally battered for five months had taken a toll. Plus, although common in California, it wasn't in Connecticut. Failure might be celebrated in commencement addresses, but it was whispered at cocktail parties. A professional death sentence you had to fight to overcome.

Julio pulled up in a stretch SUV– enough room for all of us. First stop– dog terminal. We waited what felt like a hundred years. A single elderly woman picked up her grunting bulldog. A young couple retrieved their puppy labradoodle. We were the only ones left. Twenty minutes elapsed. Finally, a thirty-something dude with a goatee came out. "I'm sorry you've been waiting to so long," he said, "One of your dogs had a rough flight and there was a lot of blood in the crate." My eyes nearly popped out of my head.

"Gordo go back now and see what is going on," I commanded. He was a step ahead of me.

"No. Sir, please. stay here. The vet is wrapping his paw."

Gordo was about to storm through the swinging doors marked *Do Not Enter* sign just as the vet emerged with both dogs on leashes. Floyd lurched toward us. Zezu limped aggressively. I sat on the ground. Pet them both. "I'm so sorry," the Delta vet said. "I think the turbulence was upsetting. He's fine but the nail did break very close to the quick so you may want to get him checked tomorrow. They are cleaning the crate. It should be ready in a few minutes."

Gordo took the leashes from her. "Thank you so much. We are going to donate the crates to you," Gordo replied. "We will not be needing them again. Have a good day." And with that, the six of us marched and limped out to the turf park for a quick walk before heading home.

Much to Julio's chagrin the dogs did not go in the back. Floyd laid on Luke's feet. Zezu draped his sixty-five-pound body in my lap. After apologizing and consoling them profusely, I settled my gaze out the window. The landscape vibrated with newness even in the grey of late December. Green signs heading north on the Merritt Parkway were now talismans– beloved counterpoints to another life in which El Camino Real marked the way home. Winding roads. Meandering stone walls. Barren winter trees gathering strength in their roots– it all spoke to me differently now. It landed us. Held us. No longer around us; but inside us. Julio dropped us at my sister Tina's house.

They were in Europe, so we had three nights to ourselves before we moved into the rental. Comforted by family pictures. Surrounded by memories of poker games and pickle-ball tournaments. That night, I climbed into their guest room bed. Slipped under the cozy down comforter. "Have you still not heard anything back from Canna Bliss?" I asked placing my head on the pillow.

"Nothing," Gordo replied. He changed into a t-shirt, "But I did reach out to their lead investor. Told him I thought he might be interested in why I resigned before they release the final twenty million tranche in January."

I widened my eyes, "Yikes, that's a bold move," I said.

Gordo smiled, "He responded immediately. We're meeting tomorrow at his office. It's a few blocks from Grand Central."

The next morning, we woke up early. I brought Gordo coffee while he got dressed. "Are you sure this is a good idea?" I asked.

"We'll see," he replied, "But something needs to tip the scales. The stalemate has gone on too long." He held up two blazers.

"Definitely the suede one," I said. "Isn't Dirk is going to flip out?" I asked nervously.

"My goal is to not even *have* the meeting," Gordo said. He checked his watch. Grabbed his wallet, "Can't miss this train," he said.

"Wait, what do you mean not *have* it?" I asked following him down the stairs.

"I'll tell you when I get home. Wish me luck." He kissed me on the forehead and was gone. I kept busy. Drew up alternate floorplans for where the furniture could go in the rental. Reached out to headhunters regarding freelance work. Nervously checked the clock. Two hours later Gordo called.

"It worked," he said, "I got to their midtown office and texted a picture of my visitor badge to Sean, Canna Bliss's lead counsel. He called immediately."

I sank back into the couch relieved beyond belief. "Wow, that is brilliant. What did he say?" I asked.

"Let's settle this. What do you want? He knew Dirk couldn't justify losing twenty million to the board no matter how much he hates me. I told him I wanted three months' severance and to be absolved of all future lawsuits or financial retaliation in perpetuity."

I smiled and nodded. "Sheer genius," I said. "Did he agree to it?" I asked.

"He did," Gordo replied, "Just said I needed to exit the lobby, cancel the meeting, and sign an NDA. I told him as long I had a contract and funds wired by end of day that wouldn't be a problem. If not, I'd be back in those offices tomorrow." Miraculously, the nightmare appeared to be over.

"Did you talk to Blake? He must be very proud of you," I said. Gordo laughed, "He was, but told me not to uncork the champagne until it's a done deal." Five hours later it was. We went into town for a celebratory dinner. I drove. Gordo called Dave to thank him for introducing us to Blake. We sent them each an annual monthly delivery of high-end craft scotch. The saga was finally over.

New Year's Eve, the boys went to Westport, out-of-their-minds excited to spend the night with friends. We stretched out on the oversized couch, wrapped ourselves in cozy chenille blankets and researched pre-owned hybrids. Gordo negotiated over text with a Midwest dealer trying to clear out inventory before year's end. By midnight we had purchased an SUV and sedan. "They'll be delivered in a week," Gordo announced triumphantly. New Year's Day we picked up the boys and moved into our rental. It felt like Déjà-vu. Gordo directed the movers on what went where. I made beds and tackled the kitchen. Luke and Finley unpacked their rooms. That evening, we picked up milk, cereal, protein powder, and school supplies at CVS. Ordered pizza for dinner and went to bed exhausted but happy.

The next day, Luke and Finley were finally going back to *their* school with *their* friends. I made protein waffles and shakes while they got ready. "Breakfast is on the table," I yelled up.

"Thanks Mama," Luke yelled back. It was good to hear his voice cheerful again. I stepped into our new sunken dining room. Stared up at the colonial brass chandelier over to the white picket fence separating the room. Luke bounded down the stairs and sat beside me. Reached for syrup across the table. It wobbled.

"Just like old times," he said smiling.

I rolled my eyes, "Wayfair never sent the part so now we have a fun little reminder of our adventure," I joked.

Luke sipped his shake. Looked up at the living room ceiling, "Hey, what are those big can things?" he asked.

"That, my boy, is some ultra-fine 1980's track lighting. All the rage back in the day."

Just then, a stinkbug landed on the table. I coerced it onto Luke's paper towel and set it free outside. "If you don't put them outside, you'll save them the return trip," Luke informed me. "It's not rocket science. Where would you rather be? Warm house or bitter cold?" he asked.

"Well, would you rather starve to death?" I argued.

"Then freeze to death?" Luke asked, "Yes. No question, Plus, don't worry, there's plenty of dead spiders in the corners they can eat." He finished his last bite of waffles, got up and with cavalier teenage certainty said, "You're not doing them any favors. You may very well be crushing their dream for a better life. I love you. We've got to get the bus."

Finley barreled downstairs. "Love you," he said. "Love you both," I said. One slam and they were gone. Sometimes, the whoosh of life takes your breath away.

Recruiting a German Nanny for Crisis Control

Our new temporary dwelling was another waiting room. I am a practical epistemologist. Meaning grounds me. As I put on rubber gloves to clean the bathroom, I wondered why we were *here–* in this 70's condo-style, pee-yellow rental with vertical blinds. We could have been home if the renters had left. I believe everything happens for a reason. That the universe is working *for us.* Obstacles are opportunities waiting to be discovered. But as I started scrubbing the sticky black-hair infested drawers, I failed to find the higher meaning. Midway through, I went downstairs to reheat my coffee. We'd left hell to live in limbo. A definite upgrade, but far from *happily ever after.*

The ice maker groaned out a few more ice cubes. Leftover Direct TV boxes and *Not to Be Thrown Out* (or apparently put away) tangle of wires and extension cords sat below the window. Outside– a yellow sea of forklifts, bulldozers, and excavators sat quiet next door. The symphony of jack hammers and back hoes would start up soon. I put my coffee in the microwave. As I watched the numbers on the digital screen countdown, I had an epiphany. Maybe the reason we were *here,* was to process what had happened. Like being in customs after leaving the country. We needed to be cleared before moving on to what would come next. The experience had changed us, but it would take time to figure out how. Had we gone back to our real home– we would have slipped back into our old life instead of creating a new one.

Comfort breeds complacency. We didn't want to be living in this weird *no man's land,* but over the weeks that followed, it gave us a chance to start fresh. Create new rituals instead of returning to old routines. Gordo started spin classes with me. We found a new coffee place. He met with finance guys on dog walks for new business ventures and worked with his partners to re-imagine the ad agency. I took a creative director job in healthcare. Great people. Generous salary. The office was in midtown, but I could work form home. The assignments were uninspiring– but I was just grateful to be working. Sundays, we went to MOMA for art and Bubby's for brunch.

Things were running smoothly until the family renting our house decided to move in full time. Test out the suburbs for real. Their non-stop issues became our full-time nightmare. Managing them directly proved challenging. We needed a buffer. Spam King was always too busy to reach out directly. He had an assistant. We needed one too. So, we created a virtual one– named her Marta. She communicated with Spam King's assistant via text from her hot pink Samsung phone. The ruse amused us, and the anonymity saved our sanity.

We considered a variety of names: upbeat Veronica, nasty Nancy, aloof Adrianna, and persnickety Penelope but ultimately landed on mighty Marta. We delighted in our highly effective new team member. She was like a strict German nanny who'd switched careers to protect overworked couples from predatory blowhards. We debated how she should sign her correspondence. Rejected *Cheers* as too friendly, *Best* as too American– ultimately opting for *Regards* which had an undeniable indifference about it. If she was feeling double-07-spunky, she signed off –M. Her notes were pleasant but perfunctory. Marta handled a mind-blowing range of five alarm fiascos from *The Horrible Middle of the Night Clanking*

Catastrophe a.k.a. baseboard heat to *The Gas Line Emergency Outage,* to which Marta called the Fire department only to discover their idiot son had turned off the bright red switch marked: NEVER TURN OFF THIS SWITCH.

Best of all was *The Emergency Pet Turtle Rescue Mission.* One Sunday night his assistant texted that their pet turtle had gotten loose and was lost in the house. They wanted to go back to the city and requested we call our housekeeper Monica to go look for it and return it via car service. Unfortunately, they'd fired her after she sent us pictures of mouse turds in kitchen drawers, gum stuck to floorboards and spoiled food in couch cushions. Marta graciously agreed to the reptile reconnaissance mission while strategically copying paragraphs 2a and 5b from the contract prohibiting non-approved pets on premise and requiring weekly cleanings by Monica. Paper trails provide contingencies. Navigating nightmares was nothing new. The renters were relentless. Marta was a lifesaver.

I found myself thinking about her *other life.* What she did when she wasn't working for us… How she ate marmite toast for breakfast. Took black tea breaks mid-afternoon. Was disgusted by the idea of exercise but remained rail thin despite eating chocolate bon bons. How she went clubbing with girlfriends after work. Preferred vibrators to dating. Read historical fiction and sang lead soprano in her church's choir. I wanted to be that bold. That devil-may-care, come-what will. Instead, I whole-heartedly committed to naming stinkbugs, giving them back-stories, and letting them stay indoors– dream of a better life.

Saved by a School Algorithm and Men in Blue

Gordo and I continued to dodge bullets, but the boys were thriving. Luke was voted co-captain of his lacrosse team, dating a great girl and out with his buddies all the time. Finley no longer had to worry about the bully kid whose dog attacked him since the boy was now in private school. He loved his classes and had a great resource teacher who helped him manage his workload. They were both back on track. Then, one night, at 3AM there was a knock on our door. Flashing police lights outside our bedroom window. I panicked. We'd seen Finley go to bed. Had he gone out? Car accident? Drugs? Had Luke been hurt? Gordo threw on a pair of jeans and hurried downstairs. I checked their rooms. Both in bed.

Gordo opened the door. Two police officers greeted him. I tried to listen from the top of the stairs but couldn't hear anything. He looked up at me, "Please get Luke. The police need to speak with him," he said. I raised my hands to ask why. Gordo shook his head no.

I opened Luke's door. "Luke honey," I said quietly. He jostled and looked up startled. "The police are here, and they need to speak with you." He stared at me, sprung out of bed, and went downstairs. Gordo opened the door and stood beside him.

"Just your son," the officer said.

Gordo stepped inside. My heart sank. He looked at me, terrified and resolute. We always stand by each other. Luke was on his own. Minutes elapsed. *What could they possibly be saying to him that we couldn't we be a part of it? Is this where our lives would change forever?*

Luke walked back in the house and sat on the stairs. "Are you okay?" I asked.

"I'm fine," he replied. Gordo put his hand on Luke's shoulder. "I'm fine dad," he said. Gordo stepped outside to speak with the officers.

Luke clenched his jaw. "I'm sorry this had to wake you," he stated curtly. His posture was guarded: his eyes sad. I put my arm around him. I didn't know what 'this' was– just that he was alive and in my arms.

"We haven't been spending enough time together, so this is kind of perfect," I said leaning my head on his shoulder. He rested his head against mine. This simple reciprocal gesture broke my heart. Gratitude exploded inside me. "I love you," I said, tears streaming down my cheeks.

"I love you too Mama," he replied, his voice softer now.

Gordo came inside, sat on the stairs, and hugged us both. "I love you Luke," he said.

"I love you daddy. Is it ok if I get something to drink and you tell mom what happened." Gordo nodded.

"Absolutely," he said. Luke went into the kitchen. I looked at Gordo. "They were responding to a self-harm alert the school algorithm picked up at 3:01."

I shook my head in disbelief, "They were here by 3:10," I said incredulously.

Gordo continued, "Apparently Luke wrote in his school computer that *it all seemed pointless, and he wished he could just die.*" I stared at the floor in shock. Tried to retrace the past few weeks for signs I should have seen. "They needed to speak with him separately to see if there was any domestic disturbance that may have caused this. Or anything going on at school he didn't want us to know about– anything he might feel more comfortable sharing with them." I nodded– understanding, but not.

We were so close. Why wouldn't he have talked to me? Probably didn't want to burden us. Probably thought he was just supposed to feel better- now that we were back in Connecticut. But, of course, he needed time to process everything that had happened. It wasn't just a door that could be closed. And it was bigger than California. I thought back to the kids that had bullied him in elementary school. How he'd come home crying. Didn't want to go to school. Childhood is brutal.

Gordo and I watched the police car back down the driveway. "These two officers left their homes in the middle of the night to protect a teenage boy they don't even know because of technology," I said.

"Mind-blowing," Gordo replied. This invisible web had caught Luke before he fell too far.

We walked into the kitchen. "I'm so sorry you are suffering," I said.

Luke stared at the counter. "I should never have written about it," he replied frustrated, "Google suggested journaling. "Obviously, a horrible idea." He looked up at us. "I would never actually *DO* anything. I just don't see the point in any of it."

Gordo looked troubled. "Any of what?" he asked. Luke turned to me, his blue-green eyes searching for help. He knew I knew what he meant. We'd talked about it. I felt it too sometimes.

"It's hard to describe," I said to Gordo, "It's less about *what*– more about *why*." I looked at Luke, "Is that what you mean?" I asked, "I don't want to put words in your mouth."

Luke nodded, "Pretty much," he replied, "but it's also the pressure of everything. Lacrosse, grades, parties– all of it."

Gordo leaned across the counter, held Luke's hand, "We love you," he said, "This happening tonight– is a good thing. I know it doesn't feel like it now."

Luke rolled his eyes. "A really embarrassing thing," he responded yawning.

"I think we should call it a night. Get some sleep," I said. We went upstairs. "Is it ok if I stay with you for a while?" I asked Luke. He nodded. Gordo blew me a kiss. Luke got into bed. I sat next to him. Rubbed his back. Brushed his hair with my fingers. Loved him until he fell asleep. Stayed with him through the night.

The next morning was Sunday. I made bacon and eggs. Luke woke up late. "Let's sit in the sunroom," I said handing him a plate. We set our breakfast on the coffee table. "We can figure out anything– but you have to let me in," I said.

His eyes filled with a swirl of sadness and relief. Then, just as quickly, they became hollow and flat. "I just don't know what the point is," he said "Nothing I do matters. I have no purpose. I wish I could just turn myself off."

I knew how he felt. "Like check out," I suggested.

"Yeah," he replied, "I would never do anything *permanent*. I just feel empty– like I go out. I go to practice. I go to parties. But the *real me* is never there. People think they know me, but they don't," he said.

"I get it," I replied, "Like you are invisible but it's better than being misunderstood or rejected."

He pushed his bacon across the plate, "Exactly and also– no matter how hard I try to do my best, it never seems like enough."

I burst out laughing. "I'm sorry," I said. "I am familiar with that feeling."

"So, what do you do about it?" he asked.

There were two roads I could go down– the PG version or the truth. If I wanted to fully understand his reality, I'd have to share my own. "Well, let me start by saying what I stopped doing. In my twenties, I used to starve myself hoping I could just disappear. Or I'd make myself sick as punishment for not being thin enough or smart enough or successful enough. In my thirties," I paused, holding my wrist, "I cut myself. Not to end anything," I assured him.

"I do that sometimes," Luke admitted, gesturing to his upper thigh, "where no one can see." My body flooded with emotion. I couldn't think. Couldn't process what he'd just said. I wanted to burst into tears, but this wasn't about me. I steeled myself against the sadness. Protected the safe space we'd created.

"I'm so sorry," I said.

"Me too for you," Luke added.

I took a deep breath. Marshalled on. "Once I committed to what I *wasn't* going to do, it opened a space for what I *could*. Does that make sense?" I asked. Luke nodded. "Okay, here's what *we* are going to do," I said making it up on the fly, "You and I like a good plan, so let's start there. First, we're going to find you a therapist."

Luke stopped me. "Can't I just talk to you?" he asked.

"I hope you do," I replied, "but some things may be easier to share with someone not in your daily life." Luke nodded. "Second," I added, "If it's ok, I'm going to call your guidance counselor and tell him the situation. Let him know you will not be in school Monday or Tuesday."

Luke's shoulders relaxed. His expression softened. "Thank you," he said.

"Today, I'd like you to do some research. Figure out one or two daily habits that will help shift your physiology or mindset. I run and meditate. Find something that feels right to you, and let's give it a shot."

Luke leaned in, "I've been watching videos of this guy Wim Hoff. His breathing method increases oxygen to the brain, and he takes ice baths to boost mood and reduce inflammation."

I nodded. "Sounds perfect," I said. "Big picture," I continued, "We are going to find something that gives you a sense of purpose. You are great at lacrosse and grades and friends, but *you* are bigger than all *that*. You have something powerful inside that needs to come out. Let's widen the lens. Figure out what you do that makes you feel ALIVE." I could see Luke's wheels turning.

"I watch a lot of motivational podcasts, mostly about athletes, who have struggled but come out on top," Luke replied.

"Great," I said "Is there something you'd want to do in that space? You're articulate and empathetic. A leader whose been through hard times. You have a lot to offer."

Luke sat up straight. "Thanks mom," he said.

"You're a powerful person, Luke. You just need to cut through all the outside static. Listen to your *inner* voice." Even as I said it, I had no idea how he'd do. Distractions were everywhere. We'd have to improvise. What came out of my mouth surprised even me. "So, we're going to go away for a few days. Change the scenery. Shift the focus. No social media. No distractions. Just you, your purpose and maybe– some sunshine."

Luke's face lit up, "Seriously?" he asked.

"Yup," I replied.

He hugged me. "I can't tell you how much this means. I love you."

I handed him his plate of cold eggs, "You may need to reheat these," I said smiling. He stood up. As he exited the room, I interjected, "Hey, do you remember what you said to me after Gran died and I told you my spirit ship felt like it was cracking into a million pieces…"

Luke looked into my eyes, "That you could stay on mine until yours came together," he said. I held my hand to my heart.

"Same," I said.

"Thanks Mama," he replied.

I missed my mom, not just for me, but the boys too. She always made time to be with them individually. After she died, I vowed to do the same. I created one-day seasonal holidays. Fall Fiesta, Winter Wonderland and Spring Fling. Pulled each boy out of elementary school for the pure joy of being together. They got to plan the day. My job was simply to relish every minute. The past few years, I'd become so focused on moving them forward, I'd forgotten how to be present. I promised myself I wouldn't micro-manage our trip. I'd make the space. Create a framework. Let Luke lead the way.

I set up a support system for when we returned. Got the name of a great therapist from Zoe. Called his coach on the DL who offered to set up weekly *Captain Walks*. That night, Luke and I discussed the trip. "Daddy booked us a long weekend to Miami. I told your guidance counselor you'd be out Friday and Monday. It's going to be a purpose quest," I said.

"That sounds amazing," Luke replied. "We *will* have fun, but this isn't a vacation," I clarified, "The point is to not to escape. It's to connect you back to *you*. To a deeper purpose. So, no social media. Only videos that feed you." I handed him a journal. "Write down what you love. What stresses you out. What passion you want to pursue. It will be a kind of roadmap for when we return. Sound good?" I asked. Luke hugged me.

Several days later we set off on our quest. On the way to the airport, Tina called. "I'm so sorry. I know you guys are in the thick of it, but Nana isn't doing well and the only assisted living place she likes just called with an opening. If she wants the room, we need to move her Tuesday. Rob and I can find a company to pack on her end. Can you and Gordo help us unpack when she arrives?" Tina asked.

"Of course. Count us in," I said.

"Thank you," she responded, "It just goes so much faster with the four of us. And I don't think I can take Nana without you."

Luke and I landed in Miami. We drove to the hotel and began our quest. He read Wim Hoff and practiced deep breathing. I bought ice bags for his baths. We wrote daily, went to the gym, sat in the sun, and ate delicious meals. Two days in, we rented bikes and cycled to South Beach. "Any revelations on your purpose project," I asked. We pedaled past bodybuilders and babes in bikinis.

"Think my purpose might be right here– in a spandex one-piece," he said.

"We could get you a full body wax to get started," I added jokingly. We biked another mile down the strip.

"I think I'd like to start a podcast called *The Breakdown*," he said.

"Sounds interesting," I replied, "What would it be about?" I asked.

"I'd interview successful people and break down the thoughts, habits and experiences that got them there." I held out my hand. He high fived it.

"Amen to that," I said.

"The focus would be on break*throughs* not break*downs*," he added smiling.

Entertaining Jail Threats and a Good Sunrise

Two days later, we moved my Nana into assisted living. Despite begging us to go there, she was now desperate to leave. Her memory was failing, her paranoia worse. She was convinced we'd tricked her into moving. The situation was complicated by the fact that regardless of her deteriorating sight, hearing, and mind, she still had power of attorney. So technically she could exit at any time. I didn't blame her for not wanting to be there but there was nowhere else to go. Old people lined the hallways eyeballing the new girl. Asking a thousand questions. She is a private introvert. "We can ask that you be left alone," I said. She turned her back to me. Kindness fueled the anger.

She stood, purse in hand, as movers brought her belongings into the room. "You take those right back out, "she demanded. "I will NOT be staying. Right NOW!! STOP bringing them in here!" She turned to me. "I will have you put in jail for kidnapping," she snarled. She'd always been a terrorist when things didn't go her way. Willing to rip you to pieces to save herself. Normally I'd walk away. Let her wear herself out, but I couldn't abandon Tina and Rob. Plus, Gordo being sick left just the three of us.

"I know this is hard Nana," I said.

"Don't you patronize me," she snapped. "You never loved me anyway. You always liked Poppop better!" The ugliness escalated. I went to hold her arm. "Don't SLAP me," she yelled, hoping someone would notice. "Please, anyone give me your phone! I need to leave," she stammered. I walked to the front vestibule to take a breath.

My brother-in-law was there directing movers. He put his arm around me. "Sorry," he said, "At least her voice still works," he added sheepishly.

"It's ok," I replied, "She's just stressed out, but I'm a little worried she may try to leave. She doesn't realize her old house has already been re-rented." The sliding glass doors opened. Movers carried in her oversized armoire. "Should we tell the guy at the front desk she is a flight risk," I asked half-kidding.

My brother-in-law laughed. "They have to buzz the residents out," he said, "So I think we should be okay." Rob didn't know her the way I did. She could be diabolical and relentless. Her husband had divorced her. Her son cut her out as soon as he turned eighteen. My mom too, long before she died.

"I'm not so sure," I said squinting to see the nameplate on the desk. "*Adam* is barely twenty and looks like he'd crack under pressure."

Rob looked over, tilted his head assessing the probabilities. He nodded "You've got a point," he agreed. "Probably a good idea." I let Adam know not to buzz her out under any circumstances.

On my way back to unpack overwrapped botanical art, the older moving guy stopped me. "She begged us to reload the truck and call her a cab," he said. His gentle eyes juxtaposed his imposing frame. I tried to imagine how this must look to him. Glimpses. That's all anyone on the outside sees. Snippets of time devoid of context. He couldn't see the 100th birthday party Gordo and I hosted for her a few months ago. Couldn't know after my third bite of broccoli she told me I'd be *a fat little piggie if I kept eating like that.* Or that she threatened to throw her plate across the room after I helped get food on her fork. All he saw was this one moment in time.

"She's feeling a bit desperate right now," I replied, "Seems to have forgotten she came here to be closer to us."

He smiled, "It must be tough being that old. She said she's a hundred," he added.

"Yup," I replied, "Just got new batteries for her pacemaker. Who knew she'd outlast them."

He smiled but looked concerned, "She said she's partly blind and deaf. Wishes the good Lord would just invite her to dinner." He didn't look away. I could feel him trying to make sense of it. *How does it get to this point? How does a lifetime lead here?* Questions lingered. Practicality prevailed.

"We were worried about her safety," I said. "That's why she's here." I hoped that he'd see we loved her and reject any ideas of aiding or abetting her exit strategies.

"Excuse me," a nurse said interrupting us, "We thought you might want to hire a full-time aid until she gets adjusted. We want to make sure she doesn't elope."

I laughed, "Elope?" I asked. I pictured Nana who hadn't had sex the last twenty years of her marriage running off to Cancun with a ninety-year-old hottie.

"Leave," she responded.

"Sorry," I said, "Elope is an odd word in this context. Let's see how she does tonight." I re-entered the room. We sliced through cardboard boxes. Tore through bubble-wrapped ashtrays, jade dragons, and boxes she'd decoupaged in her forties. Unpacked the remains of her life.

She sat on a couch in the hallway. Refused to come in. Begged every resident or nurse who passed by for money, "I'll pay you back. I just need to get out of here. Can you please call me a cab?" One after another they said, "Just give it time. It will get better."

An hour later she wandered back into the room. "It's looking nice," my sister Tina said, "We made your bed. Do you want me to show you?" She held Nana's hand to guide her.

"Don't you touch me," she scolded my sister, "I would never stay here. This place is horrible." She got up close and pointed her finger in my sister's face, "I hate you and her," she said pointing to me, "I hate all of you. Call me a cab right now. Do you hear me?" she said.

With the kindness of a saint my sister gestured to the window overlooking the garden, "It's a lovely place, Nana. Beautiful trails to walk. Great food. Kind residents." Rob and I continued unpacking. This was round seven of the same conversation.

"I will sit on the floor and scream and embarrass you," she threatened.

I laughed, "Knock yourself out," I said under my breath.

"Oh, and now you are whispering," she said.

I stood up. I'd had enough. "Tina, I'm going to go. I don't want to sit in an hour of traffic. I will come organize her clothes tomorrow."

Tina hugged me. "Thank you so much for being here. I couldn't have done this without you." Nana was still hissing her nastiness.

"I love you," I said to her as I left.

Nana threw up her arms. "So, you're just going to walk out. She always does that," she said to my sister. I walked down the hall listening to their conversation.

"She's been unpacking your things for hours," my sister said. "She brought you home-made cookies and an orchid."

I headed back to the car– my stomach, shoulders, and thoughts in knots. I was too flat-out exhausted to even cry. Tough afternoon. I was grateful to Tina and Rob for always being there. Angry at my Nana for ruining what could have been a loving time together. I looked up at the sign as I exited. I hadn't seen it on my way in. *Welcome to Sunrise* it read. I burst out laughing. *Sunrise.* The name of the assisted living center where old people went to die was called *Sunrise.* Perfect.

Kiss Dolls, Star Wars, and Exit Strategies

Spring is inevitable. Light stayed up past its winter curfew. Crocuses poked their heads through the dirt. Before long– June. We had two months left in our rental. Luke and Gordo disappeared into the armpits of Pennsylvania and Maryland for lacrosse showcases. Finley had culinary camp in the morning, football camp in the afternoon. Work for me was quiet but steady.

Mid-month, there was a flurry of texts between Marta and spam king's assistant. *You need to mulch the property. It is in the contract.* It wasn't. But Marta replied with her perfunctory charm. *Happy to do so when you provide keys to the locks you changed and reallow our housekeeper to clean as stipulated in the contract.* After a week of terse exchanges between assistants, Monica cleaned, and we mulched. Monica was like family. She'd been with us since Luke was born. We supported her when her children were smuggled over the Mexican border by relatives. She helped us through a two-year home renovation when we lived in the basement, washed dishes in the powder room and ate out of the microwave.

It had been a labor of love. We designed every detail. Found salvaged beams, wide-planked floorboards, and pewter doorknobs. Wainscoted walls and coffered ceilings. Gordo and the boys laid tile in our bathrooms. We painted as a family. Every inch of our home had memories and love baked into it. So, when Monica texted us pictures, we were crushed. They'd refused to let our gutter guy clear out the fall leaves, so rain had leaked through the roof in our sunroom. The ceiling sagged. The floorboards warped. Puddles filled the Belgian linen cushions of our

Restoration Hardware couch. Mouse droppings littered the kitchen drawers. Gum was ground into the wooden floors. Nails drilled into the walls for blackout blinds on every window. I felt violated and guilty. We were the caretakers of our home and we'd failed to protect her. The damage was fixable in varying degrees, but it filled me with dueling rage and grief. Monica cleaned as best she could.

"Marta is going to give them a piece of our mind," Gordo said after seeing the pictures.

"Not so fast," I replied, "We have their two months security deposit. It won't cover the damages but if they know we're upset, they may try to use it as their last month's rent which would really leave us high and dry."

Gordo rolled his eyes. "Well, that's unfulfilling," he said.

"No doubt, but *Marta* needs to stay focused on the bigger picture," I replied. Sure enough, a week later, his assistant reached out to ask when their security deposit would be returned. Marta responded: *As soon as the lease is over, so long as there isn't any damage.* Their assistant assured her there wouldn't be as they were having a professional cleaning crew come in to take care of everything. *Terrific,* Marta responded, *Then, they should have it within a week or two,* she replied. We had Monica's pictures so no half-ass cover-up job would work.

We'd been packing boxes every weekend. By early July, progress was significant. Yet, much remained to be done. One morning, I woke up supercharged. Luke and Gordo were at another tournament. "Finley are you up for power-packing with me today. Dinner anywhere you want tonight," I said.

He could see the kid in me that just wanted to get this whole packing business behind us. "Of course," he said. "Want me to DJ?" he asked.

"Yes, please!" I said excited that he was not only on board– but going to make it fun.

We packed knickknacks with Lizzo, linens with Elton John, boxed up winter clothes with Frank Sinatra and books with Bruno Mars. We taped and labeled to ACDC. Midday, we went to CVS to pick up Gatorade and more packing tape. Finley ran into an old friend he hadn't seen since elementary school. "Dude, what happened to your face," he said.

"Oh, I got attacked by a dog," Finley replied.

"Shit man are you okay?" he asked.

"Yeah, totally fine. It was a couple years ago. How are *you*?" The conversation continued. I paid. Finley and I walked back to the car.

"Does that happen a lot?" I asked.

"Sometimes," he said.

"I'm so sorry," I replied.

"It's ok. I'm used to it," he reassured me.

"But you never talk about it," I noted.

"I talk to dad. I know it's hard for you," he said putting his arm around. "Dad told me when the nightmares started again– to just talk to him."

I felt hurt, betrayed, left out– but I didn't want Finley to feel bad. And Gordo was only trying to help. They weren't wrong. I'd had panic attacks for nine months whenever any dog came toward us. "I totally understand," I said opening the car door for him, "but it's always okay to talk to me too, if you want to," I added.

"I know," he replied, "I love you Mama girl."

What should we listen to for Packathon Part Two?" he asked. We debated the attributes of Pitbull vs. Andy Grammar and Jamiroquai vs. Maroon Five. Decided to embrace it all. We packed and sang; danced and packed. At five o'clock I taped the last box and labeled it with a sharpie.

"That's a wrap. You've worked so hard. Dinner anywhere you want," I said.

"Can we just order sushi and watch *Star Wars*?" he asked.

"Sounds dreamy," I replied. We snuggled up on the couch, ate sushi, talked to each with Chewbacca accents and fell asleep– his head in my lap.

Luke and Gordo arrived late the next afternoon. "Total blow-out," Luke said, walking around boxes to open the fridge.

"Hey mom, can we order pizza. There's nothing in the house," Luke said.

"Wow, you guys packed a lot. Thanks for doing all that," Finley said sarcastically.

Startled, Luke looked around. "I'm sorry," he said, "Wow, you guys did do a ton," he said.

"You must have worked all weekend," Gordo commented.

"We did," Finley responded winking at me.

"Finley was an all-star champ. So, order pizza but make sure you get half Hawaiian for my partner," I said sitting on the box beside Finley. He put his arm around me. I looked at the results of our hard work. There were a lot of boxes but less than when we arrived. One advantage of moving is purging. Gordo is a collector. I am a discarder. He keeps everything– childhood lunchboxes, miniature KISS dolls, deflated soccer balls. I'll give away your shoes if you're not wearing them.

Three moves in one year allowed for a generous amount of editing. We'd reduced our wardrobe but doubled our furniture. We'd sell most of it but needed some of it to replace what our renters had ruined. "We have some choices to make," I announced, "Do you all want to keep your new California Nectar mattresses or use the ones in your room at home," I asked the boys.

"I don't want any part of California in my room," Luke said. "Well, except maybe for my desk and nightstand." he added smiling.

"Can I stack one mattress on top of the other?" Finley asked.

"Sure, we'll get you a ladder to climb in at night," Gordo teased. We sold or donated what we wouldn't be taking.

One week later we were finally going home. Movers arrived early and loaded the trucks. I was sweeping the empty kitchen when Gordo entered, "I have good news and bad," he said. "Good news is the renters are gone and the house is open. Bad news is our attorney called. All those letters from teachers and mutual friends testifying to Finley's sweet, dog-loving character made no difference. So, your deposition is officially scheduled five weeks from now. I'm so sorry Kels," he said. I was dumbfounded.

"I don't understand. How could she *still* feel okay saying he'd do such a thing. Much less that she *saw* it happen. I watched her walk back to the kitchen," I said feeling both outrage and defeat.

"I know. It's crazy," Gordo replied, "but we still have to prove *his* innocence in order to prove *their* liability."

I thought about what lay ahead. I'd need to recreate the entire event. Relive every bloody detail. I stared at the pile of crumbs in the middle of the floor. Angrily swept them into the dustpan. Gordo held out the garbage bag. I stare at him in utter disbelief.

"I get that their dog is a rescue. That they'd want to protect him. Dogs are family. I get that. We'd feel the same. But I *don't* get how she'd be willing to blame Finley for provoking the attack," I said finally dumping the dirt. Adrenalin spiked. Cortisol crashed. All the feelings came crashing back. The cognitive dissonance was deafening.

I tried to believe she was doing the best she could. Maybe their attorney told them to do it. Maybe her kids begged her not to let anything happen to their dog and she just did what needed to be done. 'Maybes' ran rampant. She was not a demon. Not my enemy. In fact, the day before I would have said she was my friend. I wanted to drive to her house. Ask why she was doing this. Beg her not to. But we were strongly advised against that.

The moving guy poked his head in the family room. "We're ready to roll whenever you are," he said.

"Let's do it," I replied. The PTSD would have to wait. Compartmentalizing had become a core competency. We walked to the door. "I have my car. I'll meet you there," I told Gordo.

"We will get through this," he said kissing me on the forehead. Everyone else left. I inspected the house to make sure we hadn't left anything. Wrote a note thanking our landlord. Left a bottle of wine beside it. It felt like Palo Alto Part Two. We'd waited seven months for this day. I was excited to go home. Yet, sad it was over. Adversity had made us closer. I didn't want to lose that when we returned to *normal* life. I stood at the front door. Addressed the empty space. *Thank you house for holding us through this time. Thank you, stinkbugs for not giving up.*

Part Five:

Going Home

Calculating the Cost of Sacrifice

My deposition for Finley's dog attack was five weeks away. I'd need to recreate what I'd tried so hard to forget. It had been three years, but the memory was clear as day… I was late for Luke's last lacrosse game of the summer season. Pick up at the library was a nightmare. Women chatting out car windows. Kids walking aimlessly across the parking lot. I spotted Finley. Waved frantically. He meandered over with his friend Mia.

"Hey, can we give her a ride," Finley asked. Ugh. We were new in town, so I didn't want to be rude.

"Hop in," I said. "Mia, are you looking forward to starting middle school," I asked.

"I guess," she replied glued to her phone.

"Your house is on Lone Pine, right? I asked.

"Yeah," she said flatly. The subtext was clear. Drive; don't talk. No matter. It was a short ride. Finley chatted on about how nice the lady teaching the class was– how she grew green zebra tomatoes using eggshells. We pulled around the small cul-de-sac. I remembered the house once we got there– new construction plunked on a postage stamp. I got out of the car and escorted Mia to her door. Rang the bell. I'd met Nora a couple times. She could be chatty, so I was nervous about keeping it brief.

I could see her approaching, cell in hand. *Great,* I thought. *Credit for the drop-off. Quick exit.* Their scrappy-looking terrier lurched at the sidelight window barking ferociously. She cracked the door open, "Don't worry," she said holding her phone to the side, "Gizmo just barks a lot. Thanks for driving." She headed back toward the kitchen. Mia followed her in. I headed to the car. Halfway there, I heard Finley joking around with Mia's little sister. He didn't realize we were in a rush. I turned around to hurry him up. As I did, Finley bent down to pet Gizmo. Time froze. The energy went ice still. Something about Gizmo was terribly wrong. I could feel it. Something bad was going to happen.

Finley had not yet pet Gizmo when I yelled, "STOP!" To the dog. To Finley. To Mia's sister. To God. To anyone who could help. I was too far away to do anything. Gizmo leapt at Finley, latched his jaws onto Finley's face and didn't let go. I ran to him. Nora slowly walked out of the house out.

"Get him off," I screamed. Nora stood still. "GET HIM OFF," I screamed again. I was now right there but terrified if I tried to rip Gizmo off, he might take Finley's face with him. Or attack me and I'd be unable to Finley. Finally, Nora ripped Gizmo off his face. Blood gushed. Finley lay on their bluestone entry shaking, crying– terrified. I put my arm around him. Helped him up "We're going to be ok," I told him, not at all sure that was true. "Nora, call 911," I said, "Get ice and towels." She stood still.

So, I took charge. Helped Finley to the kitchen. Grabbed ice myself. Wrapped it in towels. "Did you call 911?" I asked.

"What do you want me to tell them?" she inquired.

I grabbed her arm. Tried to jolt her back into reality. "Tell them there has been a dog attack. We need an ambulance immediately." She just stared at me. "Nora– PLEASE" I begged. My cell was in the car.

"Where should I tell them to go," she asked. There was blood all over the floor. Was she on Valium? Give them your address," I said. But I knew Finley and I were on our own. He was shivering now, his teeth chattering from the trauma. He clutched the ice towel to his eye. "Let's go get help honey," I said. We walked to the car. As we got to the curb, I heard sirens.

A neighbor ran up to us. Life clicked back into real time. "I saw it all. Horrifying," she said breathless, "I called for an ambulance. I am going to text you the name of a great plastic surgeon. Give me your number." I did. Fire engines, police and an ambulance arrived. The rest is a blur. Once I knew help was there, fear flooded my body. I assisted Finley to the ambulance.

An EMS paramedic ushered me into the truck. He had Finley sit facing the opposite direction. He put his hand on Finley's shoulder, "Can I take a look at your eye buddy?" he asked. Finley removed the bloody towels. "See if you can follow my hand," he said calmly. He moved his hand to the right, then to the left, then up and down. He asked Finley a few questions I can't remember, then smiled and said, "You are going to be okay." He turned to me and in a lower voice said, "He did not lose his eye. Or his sight." Tears of gratitude streamed down my face. "But he did lose a large piece of cheek right below his left eye down to his ear. He will need plastic surgery."

I held Finley close on the way to the hospital. The paramedics made small talk. Kept Finley engaged with their kindness. He was in shock, not yet aware of what the coming hours, weeks or years would bring. I texted Gordo who was half an hour away at a lacrosse tournament with Luke. They left immediately. Finley entered the hospital in a blur. We were ushered into an ER room. They took Finley's vitals. I found the neighbor's text. Quickly googled the plastic surgeon she'd recommended. He was highly regarded. I asked the nurse if we could use him. "He doesn't work out of this hospital. The surgeon on call is Anya Kishinevsky. She is an excellent surgeon. Given the extent of the damage we need to contact her immediately. Otherwise, you'd need to take him to another hospital. I'll give you a minute to decide." Just then Gordo and Luke arrived. Luke hugged Finley. Gordo and I researched the surgeon on call. She had reconstructed a child's face after the infamous Stamford chimpanzee attack. She was the one.

Twenty minutes and two police statements later, she arrived. Took charge immediately. Introduced herself to us and addressed Finley directly. "It would be best not to wait for the general anesthesiologist but that means we will need to administer two local numbing shots very close to your eye. They *will* hurt but the surgery *won't*." She was kind but did not mince words, "Once I begin you cannot move at all. I cannot emphasize that enough. Are you okay with that?" she asked Finley. He looked at us.

I held his hand, put my other hand on his chest, and bent close to him, "This is totally up to you," I said, "You have been so incredibly brave." He looked at the surgeon and nodded. "Are you sure?" I asked. He nodded again and squeezed my hand.

She prepared the needles, then turned to us, "Mom and dad, you are going to have to hold him down so there is no movement."

"Okay," we said. We pinned his shoulders to the bed. He stared at us terrified.

"Ready," she said. We nodded.

She stuck the long needle into his temple. He screamed at the top of his lungs. I wanted to strike her. Hold him. Stop the insanity. She removed the first needle. Picked up the second. "Please Mama, No more. PLEASE!" Finley screamed.

"Wait," I yelled. She stopped. "Is there any cream or anything that can numb the area before the second shot?" I asked.

"No," she replied. She waited. I looked at Finley hysterically crying, begging me to make her stop.

"I love you honey. We are halfway there," I said, tears now streaming down my face. I nodded at our surgeon to go ahead. Betraying your child to save them is unbearable.

Throughout the long surgery, Gordo and I held Finley's hands. Luke stood at the end of the bed, holding his foot. Twenty minutes in, she removed half the stitches she'd just sewn. I looked at Gordo. "It is a large gap we are closing between his upper and lower cheek. Close to two inches. We need to make sure it doesn't pull the corner of his eye down or it will be disfigured. I am going to restitch it to prevent that."

I took a deep breath, "Thank you," I said trying not to sound nervous or terrified. She finished forty-five minutes later. It still looked gruesome but her precision instilled confidence.

"I will see you in a couple days," she said to Finley, "Stay inside. No activities. Be as still as possible. The nurse will bandage you up. You did a great job." She pulled Gordo and me into the hallway.

I didn't want to appear ungrateful, but his eye still dragged dramatically down at the corner. "Will the shape of his eye return to normal?" I asked.

"Yes," she said "It *won't* look this way when it is healed but it *will* appear worse in the next few days. That is part of the healing process. It will improve in the coming weeks. This is going to be a long road and he may need a revisionary surgery, but he's a lucky boy. One inch over and he would have lost his eye. The nurse will be here in a few minutes to bandage him up," she said.

We re-entered the room. "Can I see what it looks like?" Finley asked. It was red, swollen, crude– garish.

"How about we let it heal a little first," Gordo suggested.

"It's my face," Finley said, "I have a right to see it." He went to the adjacent bathroom. Came out crying. "I look like a monster," he said.

Luke put his arm around him, "Dude, I think it looks like a Nike swoosh."

A month passed. The stitches were removed. The red ropiness remained. We did twice daily gentle massages with scar cream, got steroid injections and kept it covered it with bandages.

The first day of middle school Finley got off the bus crying. We walked down our street away from the other kids. "They all made fun of me," he said, "Called me a dog attacker. Told me I was a faker."

I put my arm around him, horrified. "That is not okay. Not at all. Honey, did Mia say this?" I asked.

"No, all her girlfriends, mostly Pam. She's the most popular girl in the grade," Finley replied.

"I love you so much. I am so, so, sorry my love. I will take care of this. It will NOT happen again." We entered the house. Sat on the couch. He put his head in my lap.

"Can I please be home-schooled. *Please.* I feel like I've lost something I can never get back." I held him close.

"You have," I said, "I wish I could change that– with all my heart." Tears rolled down my cheeks onto his. "Someday this loss will become a superpower," I said.

Terrible things happen. Our family lives by a 'pivot or die' philosophy. We hurt. We heal. We come out stronger. We could get through the attack, but cruelty was different. I called Pam's mom that night. She and Nora were best friends. "I am calling regarding an extremely serious matter I am hoping we can resolve without me needing to contact the school," I said.

"What happened?" she asked. I could tell by her voice she had some idea.

"I'm sure you've heard by now Finley was attacked by Mia's dog." I waited for her to respond.

"I heard *something* happened," she replied.

I inhaled audibly. Tried to stay calm. "A horrifying, traumatic dog attack happened," I corrected her. "I don't know what Mia has told her friends, but they are accusing Finley of something he didn't do and bullying him. I'm sure you're aware the school has a zero-tolerance policy for that kind of behavior."

She responded immediately, "Yes. I do know that. I will speak with Pam about this," she said.

"Thank you," I replied. "I don't want to call the school but if it happens one more time, I will." We hung up.

Twisted Truths and Magic Shrooms

Three years later Finley's scar had faded. The reminder was always in the mirror, but he'd moved on from the memory–until I started preparing for my deposition. I tried to keep the anxiety to myself. Gordo and I talked privately. But the deposition loomed on the horizon like a dark storm cloud. Finley's nightmares returned. We found him a therapist who helped. I needed help but therapy had proven useless. No matter how hard I tried I couldn't process why Nora hadn't called 911. At the time, I'd assumed it was shock.

But I couldn't figure out why she had claimed in her police statement to have seen the attack. Why she had accused Finley of something he'd never do. None of it made sense. I knew Nora was an attorney. A child had been viciously attacked on *her* property by *her* dog. Connecticut law states: *The owner is not liable for injuries and damages sustained by someone who is teasing, tormenting, or abusing the dog.* But I still didn't get it. It's not like she'd have to pay our medical expenses. Her insurance would. Was she afraid they'd raise her rates? Surely, that couldn't be it. Nora wasn't just an attorney. She was a mother. I couldn't reconcile the cruelty.

Nora was deposed two weeks ahead of me. Our attorney sent the transcript. Contrary to her police report, she said she was in the kitchen and *hadn't* seen it. When the discrepancy was pointed out, she said she *had* seen it. Then she changed her story to say she *hadn't*. When pressed for the truth, she concluded she *had not* seen the incident but knew from her daughter that Finley provoked the attack. I called Gordo.

"You read it right?" I asked.

"Yes," he said. "I'm about to go into a client meeting so I only have a couple minutes."

"Surely, that absolves Finley of fault," I replied getting straight to the point.

"Unfortunately, no, but there *is* good news. Apparently, she is refusing to have her children testify, so if you do well in your deposition, they will likely change strategy and admit liability." I was silent for a second.

"Strategy is how you pack a dishwasher or play checkers. Flip-flopping on whether to accuse a child of something he didn't do is something quite different," I replied.

"I totally agree," Gordo said.

"So, our strategy is what– just smile and nod?" I asked.

"Unfortunately, not far off. I called my friend Laura who used to practice on the insurance side. I can tell you more later, but in a nutshell, she said *sadness is good but make sure your wife does not come across as angry even if she is. Stick with the facts. Tell her to not add her opinion or share any theories about why the defendant may have acted the way she did.*"

"Got it," I said flatly. I could hear Gordo's assistant in the background, *They're in the conference room.* "I'll talk to you later," I said. I felt tormented, not sad. Outrage not sorrow. Nora's *strategy* had destroyed me and now I'd have to fake my feelings to protect our case. The ability to collect damages and prove Finley's innocence was in my hands.

The parameters left me powerless. Despair and rage twisted me into a knot of emotional paralysis. Gordo's attempts at consolation felt like Pollyanna platitudes. My job was to package hell into Hallmark. Normally, I can do anything. I am a Puritan pilgrim by nature. Get through it. Get over it. Get on with it. But this was different. I was drowning. I needed help. Serious help. Not talk therapy and medication. *This* was bigger than *that.* So, I called my friend Juliette. She is an intuitive. That makes logical people squirm. But logic was getting me nowhere. Juliette cuts right to the point. Doesn't ask obvious questions like: *How does that make you feel?* She travels where thought can't go. Navigates around emotions that get stuck.

"I know I am supposed to act like the grieving mother," I said, "but I am angry."

"You are both," she replied, "Anger is sitting on top. But of course, you are the grieving mother." I held my breath. Anger was easier. "It's not an act," she continued, "And it's not your fault." Tears popped out fully formed. "You and Finley have lost something beyond what you can see," she said, "This is your chance to get it back. It's not about a settlement. It's about reclaiming your voice. Speaking the truth," she said.

I clenched my jaw. "They aren't there for the truth," I replied, "They are going to trick me, twist my words, try to frame Finley for attacking their dog." I started to feel light-headed.

Juliette was quiet. "This is bigger than the deposition or the dog attack," she said slowly. I could feel her channeling. After a long pause she said, "Don't think I'm crazy but you need to do mushrooms." I burst out laughing. Nothing breaks through fear like humor.

"You mean like Shitake or Morrel," I asked. "Because if you're suggesting I start shrooming– let's just say I am *not* a good candidate."

She laughed. "Got it. No, not *shrooming*," she said, "But– yes psychedelic mushrooms. Micro-doses. Not enough to trip. Just to open your mind. Let out what doesn't need to be there."

Clearly, she didn't know what I meant by *not a good candidate*. "My imagination is already on acid. I'm too wired to do cocaine. Marijuana makes me want to set up my own witness protection program. I barely even drink."

She was silent. "You're serious?" I asked.

"I know," she said, understanding my apprehension. "I had the same response, but yes. Psilocybin mushrooms saved my life. You know about my brain aneurisms. Since I started taking them–my MRI scans are totally clear. Mushrooms are powerful healers. Our government criminalized them, but other cultures have been using them for centuries."

"Seems a bit extreme," I replied.

"The attack is triggering issues you've suffered with your whole life. This is a chance to transcend them," she responded. I paused.

"I'll send you articles," she added, "Watch the movie Fantastic Fungi. It will blow your mind."

Was it really coming to this? Drugs? I'd tried everything else. Psychologists, EMDR and biofeedback. Metaphysical theology and Reiki. Not to mention the full gamut of SSRI's, MAOI's and over-the-counter supplements. Even colonoscopies in case it was all trapped there. But never mushrooms.

"I'll watch the movie," I said, and then thinking ahead, "I'm guessing they aren't available at CVS." She laughed. "Do you have someone I can get them from," I asked.

"Let me reach out to my contact Mack and see if it's okay to put you two in touch." I was strangely excited. At fifty-three, this would be my very first drug deal. *Potential* drug deal. The deposition seemed light years away. I had no idea how mushrooms would help but I felt hopeful.

Getting Past Penis Envy and Alligators

I go by gut. Throw away Ikea directions. Eyeball couch assembly. The reasons to run were glaringly obvious. But mushrooms kept cropping up. Tim Ferris raved about their ability to treat therapy-resistant trauma. *The New York Times* reported about how they helped vets with PTSD. Mushrooms had even come up at a recent cocktail party in connection with the Peter Thiel-backed psychedelic start-up ATAI Life Sciences. Now, Juliette. I watched the *Fantastic Fungi* movie. Turns out, mushrooms were the future of pretty much everything. The benefits were vast and undeniable. A Yale study linked them with improved behavioral responses to chronic stress. I'd use them to prepare for the deposition. Give them to Gordo for migraines. Heck, if they worked, maybe I'd give them to Finley for focus. Luke for hopelessness. They'd cure our family. Maybe the world.

Juliette sent Mack's number. I composed the text a few times. Mentioned that she suggested I call him about… umm, well… I settled on *help moving forward*. Left out any incriminating references. Right then, I had that first uh-oh feeling. Like the time Gordo and I took the boys horseback riding up a semi-active volcano in Guatemala to roast marshmallows. I could frame it anyway I wanted, but what I was about to do was a federal crime. There was no free pass for 'using' narcotics to relieve emotional stress. I suddenly started getting paranoid. Every text, google search and email was recorded. The government could access anything– use it to prosecute anyone at any time. I sent the text anyway. And when Mack called, I answered.

I imagined him like a pharmacist. Gave him a topline about my post-traumatic stress and hope for peace of mind. Tried not to overshare but also give him enough information to prescribe the right type of mushroom. He didn't *seem* like a drug dealer. What did they seem like? I had no idea. But not him. He was soft-spoken. Informative. Not pushy. Regardless, I *did* have a list of questions. I'd ask them in my most *laid-back, convo-with-a drug-dealer* tone but *chill* is not one of my stronger qualities. I didn't want to scare him. I didn't imagine drug dealers like to be grilled. But I *did* need some answers. He began referencing what I thought might be acronyms–but he had a strange habit of dropping syllables so I couldn't make out what he was saying.

It made me uncomfortable. Not like breathing in skinny jeans after lasagna. More like you could fry your brain or rot in jail for misunderstanding. I began freaking out. I didn't want to come across as stupid or defensive or difficult, but I had to speak up. My 'take charge' approach can sometimes come across like a fire hose trying to extinguish a candle, so, I tried to be low-key. "Mack, I was just wondering what benefits they provide, suggested dosing, possible side effects and time for onset?" There was a long pause. I *might* have asked too many questions, too quickly. *Great*, I thought. *I've blown it.* The deal is going to go south before it even gets off the ground.

Mack responded slowly, "Based on what you said you're looking for… I would send .5 of the JAM and .5 of the TAT. Start with one every two to three days and don't eat for three hours before." TAT? JAM? What WAS he talking about? I'd made a list of slang names and binomial nomenclature. These were nowhere on it. He's probably just short handing it, I told myself. It's not like I was going to take some random concoction he whipped up in his basement… *right?*

I looked at the mushroom type I'd circled as most likely to be right for my issues. Wished it had a different name. "Um, Mack, so, is JAM part of the *Penis Envy* strain," I tried to ask casually.

"No, neither of these is Penis Envy," he replied.

I was open to ingesting random drugs from a guy I'd never met. I was just hoping for a modicum of reassurance. I decided to take a different tactic. I slid my list of questions across the dining room table. "Mack, I've got to be honest, I've never done drugs. I have no idea what any of this means. How did you educate yourself on all this, so you'd know what was– what."

He softened a bit. "I've been doing it for thirty years. Self-taught." he said. This would be a total leap of faith. No nutritional labels or return policy. I could go with it or get off the phone.

"So, it was more of an experiential education," I said hoping for just a little more.

"Exactly," he said. Relaxed by the apparent end of interrogation, he continued. "I live on a cattle farm, so I grow them there. Cow dung is a great fertilizer." I put my head in my hands. "I am a nature person," he continued. "Used to train wild exotic animals. Crocodiles and alligators. I was on a National Geographic episode called *King of the Swamp.* You can look it up." There it was– the turning point. In a normal job interview, this would have been a reference. Not a terribly relevant or even remotely related one. But in the world of drug dealings perhaps this was the best it got.

"Let's do it," I said.

"How much do you want," he asked.

"A month's supply," I said. Figured I'd share with Gordo.

There was a pause. "Okay," he replied, "Are you sure you want that much to start? That would be," he paused– I imagined doing the math on some nearby envelope, "Thirty of the TAT and eight of the JAM. Would come to three hundred twenty-one dollars. Is that okay?"

My mind raced with the endless ways in which this was definitely NOT okay. "Yes," I replied. Figured go big or go home. Moderation isn't in my DNA.

"Venmo me one hundred now. I will send it tomorrow. You must refrigerate them once opened. When you get the package, please mail the balance in cash" he said.

He must be kidding, I thought. What if it gets lost or he denies having received it? He seemed nice but this was the part where people would come after me later. "Can I Venmo you the rest," I asked. "I just don't want it to get stolen."

There was a pause. "It won't," he said. "I do this all the time. Just wrap it in paper." Gordo was listening from the kitchen. He hurried in– gave me two thumbs up and an overstated head nod. I raised my hands in the '*are you kidding, this is crazy*' gesture.

He whispered, "He can't have a trail." I looked dubious. He scribbled on my paper: IT'S OK. GO WITH IT.

"Okay," I confirmed. Nothing about this was okay. The sleeplessness began that night. I was a criminal. I hadn't covered up lies since high school. *That* was fixable by more lies and an apology. *This* could involve jail time. And suburban disgrace. The children's lives would be ruined. I'd be forced to eat prison slop, get dragon tattoos, and become somebody's bitch. Eventually, I'd perish of malnutrition and the children would be raised motherless. I could still stop 'the deal'. But I didn't. Just knowing a box of TAT and JAM was headed my way gave me hope. Mushrooms felt safer than medication. At least they didn't come with a laundry list of side effects. I preferred the idea of short-term micro-dosing to long-term pill-popping.

I'd never done hard-core drugs. The closest I'd come was a medically administered ketamine infusion I'd tried to transcend old traumas and reach higher l consciousness. I contacted a company called Field Trip. The name seemed a little kitschy. Field trips usually result in poison ivy, not personal epiphany but I was desperate. They had *guides* to assist clients on fifty-minute *trips* to help integrate whatever came up. I liked the controlled environment and limited timeframe in case I didn't respond well. I did the medical intake forms, had my consultation call and a week later, Gordo drove me to their midtown Manhattan location. The place had an upscale urban opium den meets google rec room vibe.

The receptionist was almost as prickly as the cactus next to her. "I will give you the tour," she said walking out from behind the desk. She gestured to the right, "This is the art therapy room. You *can* sit on the poofs but *not* the futons because we have an important group coming in later." We passed the kitchen. "This is the client snack room," she said to me. Then looking at Gordo, "There is a deli across the street if you're hungry." She pointed out the zero-gravity chairs, noise-cancelling headphones, curated playlists, and weighted blankets. The whole place felt like an elaborate stage-set. Like you could come back tomorrow, and it would be a dentist office.

The experience itself started out fine. A lovely nurse took my blood pressure and explained what would be happening. Ten minutes after being injected, I began losing control of my muscles. My body turned to concrete. I couldn't speak. Couldn't move. It felt like I was being stripped of free will. Injected with amnesia. Like I was entering *The Bourne Identity*, but it wasn't a movie, and I wouldn't come out alive. I thought about all the release forms I'd signed. I remained in full panic mode for half an hour. When it finally wore off, my *guide* brought me strawberries and a can of mango Kombucha tea to help recovery.

"Sometimes these sessions can bring up a lot of issues," she said noticing my agitated state.

"It brought up absolutely nothing. I spent the entire session unable to move. It was the opposite of therapeutic," I replied.

"Have you felt that *paralyzed* feeling before," she asked. Her question embodied everything I hated about therapy.

"No, never," I responded flatly.

"We can set up a follow-up session if you'd rather talk about it later," she offered.

I declined. She left. The nurse returned to check my blood pressure. "Just so you know," she said softly, "Ketamine *is* anesthesia, just in a low dose, so that may have been why you couldn't move." I thanked her. Went to the client room. Stuffed my purse full of mediocre snacks for Gordo and we left. Not a great entry into the world of narcotics, but mushrooms were organic. Plus, I was only taking a micro-dose. Not so much I'd hallucinate. Just enough to release the trauma.

Navigating Brain Fog and Ego Death

Mack's package arrived as promised within a couple days. The capsules were vacuum sealed, and triple wrapped in unmarked grey plastic bags. The kind readily available in third world bodegas. No note. No directions. One marked TAT. The other JAM. Seemed a bit Alice in Wonderland-y, but Sunday came, and Gordo and I popped the pill. We sat in our sunroom. Early morning light filtered through the trees. Flickered across the grey linen couch. Gordo was talking about the generational implications of *The Morning Show* when I thought I might vomit.

The room tipped side to side like a ship in a storm. It felt like someone had remote-hacked my brain and was using a cursor to move my thoughts. Gordo assured me it would pass. He had experience with drugs. "Just give it 15 minutes," he said. Fifteen felt like fifty. Even after it passed, I felt terrible.

"My brain feels like thick fog. I don't know how I'm going to prepare for the PPT meeting tomorrow," I said.

"Maybe it's working behind the scenes. Breaking down barriers. Rewiring your mind," Gordo replied. "Well, that would be nice," I said, "Hopefully it will be rewired before we have to drive Finley to football and shop for groceries."

Wednesday came. I decided to try again. I got up early. Worked out. Ate. Waited three hours. Took half a pill. It would be a mini-micro-dose. More like a glorified multi-vitamin. No kids home. Day off work. Only one harmless ZOOM call for the refugee charity I'd recently agreed to help with marketing. I could do it off-camera on mute. One hour in– it had no effect. I considered taking the second half but decided not to get overambitious. Fifteen minutes later, it kicked in– hard. No nausea this time. Just more blindingly thick brain-fog. Zero visibility to thought. Zero ability to navigate conversation. That's okay, I thought. Maybe insight comes when thoughts slow down. I tried to stay open-minded. Right then, a text came in. *So sorry, the board needs to see a social media strategy by end of day to approve funding.* WHAT? I'd agreed to write marketing materials not strategy proposals. I didn't even know their objectives. Ugh. Cryptic direction. Tight deadline. Not good. Not at all.

Before I tackled the surprise assignment, I had to attend their 'Quarterly Status Update' ZOOM meeting. I'd been to meetings like this before. Usually, a mind-numbingly boring state of the union address wherein the founder provides excruciating detail about where the money has gone and the worthy initiatives that require more. Tedious but not interactive. So, I got a grape popsicle, tied my hair in a knot, put a lavender heating pad across my shoulders and sat cross-legged in my white office chair. I opened my laptop and clicked JOIN. Seven people's faces popped up on my screen. All live. All smiling. I panicked. What was THIS?

"Hi Kelly," the Organizer said, "I understand you are new to our team. Welcome. Before we get started, I thought we could introduce ourselves and say a little bit about what we do. Where are you from?"

Oh Lord, I thought, this is a MEET and GREET. I threw off the lavender pad. Ripped out my hair knot. Put the popsicle in my water glass. Turned my camera and microphone on. "Hi," I said feeling like a baby elephant hiding from poachers behind a

bamboo shoot. Everyone was smiling at me. Where am I from…
where am I from… Like where I've worked? Where was I born?
Where do I live now? The State? Town? Seconds were passing.

"Kelly…" she said prompting me.

"Oh, so sorry," I said, "Connecticut," I forced myself to
smile and nod. Lean in but not too far. Appear not to be in the
middle of a full-blown panic attack.

When the call ended, the spiral began. I'm great in crisis.
Bad at aftermath. I'd left my body to attend the call, but having
returned, I had no idea know where I was. I tried revising the ads,
but tears made it blurry. They'd have to wait. I texted
Juliette. *Having very bad experience. Again. Any advice?* She
responded: *Ego death is sadness is love is bliss.* I rolled my eyes.
She had to be kidding. I get that she operates in different realms,
but this was next level. You can't send postcards from sunny
Hawaii to someone stuck in a full-blown tornado. I cried. Made
revisions. Researched ego death. *Ego Death is a complete loss of
subjective identity followed by a transcendent oneness with the
universe.* I cried more. Laid down. I was soooo tired. Looked at the
clock. 2:30. I'd never get the proposal done by 5:00. I considered
writing off the whole micro-dosing experience to inhospitable
body chemistry, but I still hadn't tried JAM.

So, I called Mack. "Did you create your set and setting?"
he asked.

"Umm," I replied stalling. I had dismissed this suggestion
as frivolous.

"You know your mindset– and physical, social setting,"
he said trying to jog my memory.

"Not totally," I replied. Slowing down stresses me out. I sometimes eat fistfuls of spinach, just so I don't have to make salad dressing.

"You also might be experiencing something called ego death. Look that up," he said.

"I did," I replied. "I'm missing the transcendent oneness part." Mack was quiet. I could tell his desire to be my mushroom mentor was diminishing quickly.

That night, I discussed it with Gordo while making dinner. "I'm so sorry this has been such a nightmare for you," he said pouring pasta into the boiling water. "It's helping me sleep and I haven't gotten a migraine since we started taking it." He added a pinch of sea salt. Stirred the fusilli. "But everyone's chemistry is different. Maybe it's not right for yours," he said. I crushed garlic. Tried to shake the hopelessness.

"It *needs* to be," I replied scraping it into sizzling olive oil. My chest tightened. My throat clenched. The kitchen slipped into oblivion and my body flooded with fear. This is how IT always started. What IT was– was impossible to say. Psychotic break. Panic attack. Post traumatic crisis. It felt like a tidal wave of despair. I'd hospitalized myself twice to try and figure IT out. Combed through my childhood. I was rarely spoken to until I was 3. Ostracized and made fun of for being fat in elementary school. Pushed into lockers by mean girls in middle school. Molested by the school psychologist in high school. There *was* stuff to point to but none of it was IT. Or maybe it was ALL of it. I'd given up anorexia, bulimia, and cutting. Learned to tolerate extreme amounts of internal conflict. But I still felt paralyzed.

I stirred the garlic. Watched it turn from gold to brown. I wanted to smash the bottle of olive oil against the stove. Scream at the top of my lungs. Crumble to the floor. But no act of rebellion could translate the pain. Gordo would ask WHY I was upset. I would not be able to tell him. Not really. If you haven't been to the Grand Canyon, it's just a big hole in the ground. He'd look confused. I'd feel insane. He'd act loving. I'd feel inarticulate. Tears streamed down my face. Shriveled garlic scittered across the pan. "It's too much," I finally said, my voice trembling.

Gordo looked back from chopping cherry tomatoes. Turned off both burners. He put his arm around me. "Come on, lets' sit down. Dinner can wait." He ushered me over to the couch. I sat on the edge– unwilling to commit. "Is this about the deposition?" Gordo asked. I shook my head no. "Tell me what's going on?" he continued.

"I don't know. There's nothing to really talk about. I'm probably just over-tired," I said overwhelmed by the enormity of my feelings and failure to translate their magnitude. "I feel cornered," I finally said, "and lost and helpless– like I'm suffocating in the same oxygen everyone else uses to breathe." Gordo paused. He knew what he said next would open me up or shut me down.

"Do you remember the BB-8 robot from Star Wars?" he asked. I sat back on the couch– curious. Relieved. Empathy alone is useless. Metaphor is the way only way out.

"No," I said, "Who is he?"

Gordo continued, "He was the robot Rey finds after the crash. He has two round balls stacked on top of each other– looks like a snowman?" Gordo said trying to help me recollect.

"I don't remember," I replied.

He continued, "Well, after the crash, his antenna gets broken. He can't figure out *where* he is or *what* he's supposed to do because he's forgotten *who* he is. His frequencies have gotten all scrambled. Rey sees him struggling. Sees his antenna is bent..." Gordo's stopped, unexpectedly caught in the story. I looked into his eyes.

"She straightens it out," I said remembering.

"And he's able to process what is happening," Gordo finished. We were quiet. Illuminating darkness doesn't change it. But light is light. "We will get through this," Gordo said, "We always do." He kissed the top of my head.

Sunday October 31st, Gordo and I embarked on a Halloween JAM. Made sure to curate our set and setting. Promised not to talk about the deposition being two days away. We sat on the back deck. Elton John playlist. White and green pumpkins on the stone pillars. Back row of burning bush in full flame. "Timothy Leary has been on my mind lately," I said.

Gordo leaned forward, "Did you know John Lennon wrote *Come Together* about Leary's vision that psychedelics could help our nation break down barriers and come together." I was listening but the burgundy-green hydrangea trees were spectacular. I wanted to freeze their beauty. Keep it from fleeting.

"That's quite a vision," I replied. My thoughts began to thicken. "The JAM is turning my mind to molasses. Guess my body chemistry is in fact not fungi friendly. Think I'm going to go for a walk at the beach," I said.

"Want company?" Gordo asked.

"Thanks, but I'm going to just get quiet– see if the universe has any brilliant messages for me."

Plotting a Pipedream and Saying Goodbye

There was no trumpet. No blinding ray of light or booming voice. But navigating goose poop coming back from the beach, the universe spoke to me. *You don't need to TAKE mushrooms to find the path. They ARE the path.* It could have meant many things. But at the time, it sounded like a calling. I was supposed to be a conduit, not a consumer. A provider, not a user. Just because they hadn't worked for me, didn't mean they weren't helping millions. And what about all the people who didn't know they existed. I was supposed to provide a path. I picked up my pace, suddenly feeling a sense of purpose.

The idea bounced around my brain like a pinball. Lit it up with all the ways this idea made perfect sense. Anxiety in coastal Connecticut had reached epidemic levels. People were popping Xanax like jellybeans. Demand was high. People needed help. They just didn't know where to turn. Mushrooms were the all-natural, non-addictive answer to mental health. We'd become underground health avengers. I realized my two-week psilocybin crash course hardly qualified me as an expert and Mack was not exactly a legitimate manufacturer. BUT Gordo and I had launched billion-dollar brands from soup to nuts. We could do this.

Untappd market. No competition. Great product. Perfect opportunity. Branding would be a dream. Everyone wants to go somewhere. We'd take people to places uncharted on maps. Unreachable by therapy. Flights to psychological freedom. Vacation from the hamster wheel of anxiety. We'd upgrade mental health to mental wealth. Create a gateway to personal truth. Portal to peace. We'd call it *The Travel Agency.* The whole concept lit my entrepreneurial fire. Before I knew it, I'd arrived home.

Gordo was in his study playing guitar. I burst in, blurted out my new business venture in a whirlwind of enthusiasm. "I see the brain fog has worn off," he said, trying to digest my entirely serious, preposterous proposition. He set his guitar pick on the desk. "Can I ask what precipitated all this?" he asked careful not to squelch my idea. I relayed the universe's message. "Do you think there might be a less criminally complicit way to interpret *They ARE the path,*" he asked.

"I'm not saying there aren't details to be worked out," I admitted, "but outside of public humiliation and incarceration it seems pretty fool-proof."

Gordo smiled. "Okay, assuming we could navigate those rather large obstacles, we don't exactly have experience."

"Not true," I argued, "Our unique life experience makes us pitch perfect. You've survived an embezzling business partner, Non-Hodgkin's Lymphoma and two ex-wives. I could escape Alcatraz with a fork if I had to." He smiled at my unorthodox sales pitch.

"You have no black hoodies or dope sneakers," he said joking.

"I have zebra Gucci platforms and attitude. Different markets- different style," I replied. He strummed a few chords.

"I assume you've worked out distribution, a sales force and drug front," he said.

"As a matter of fact, I have some solid ideas," I said. "We incorporate what I think we should call, *The Travel Agency*, as a religion. Treat mushrooms as sacraments covering them under the same law that protects American Indians using Peyote. We host monthly cocktail parties we call *Services* and collect *Donations* at the door making transactions untraceable. BAM! Legal loopholes covered. AND because we'd be a non-profit, we wouldn't have to pay taxes."

"Impressive," Gordo said playing the chorus of Tom Petty's *Learning to Fly*. "Sales force?" he asked.

I sat down in his red leather guest chair. Crossed my legs. "Easy," I answered, "DTC is the new retail. Brand ambassadors–the new sales team. Zoe leads global sales for MLM vitamins, BUT she's been saying she wants to start something new."

Gordo suddenly stopped playing, "You haven't talked to her yet, right?" he asked nervously.

"I'm not an idiot," I said, "but she *has* been looking for the next big thing. This could be it." Gordo began playing again. I continued, "We recruit Dante to be Spiritual Director. You know how charismatic he is. Plus, he grew up in Baptist country so, he'd be perfect," I said.

"You figured all this out on your way back from the beach?" he asked.

"Yup. And let's not forget manufacturing," I continued, "You know your buddy Justin who gave you the mushroom chocolates last year? We hook up with his source. Curate exotic flavors like Orient Ginger Express and Black Pepper Safari to maximize The Travel Agency brand. Use sustainably sourced ingredients and electric delivery vehicles. Diversity-rich! Environmentally responsible! BAM and BAM."

Gordo nodded. "All this on a 5-mile walk?" he said dumbfounded.

"I know it's crazy, but I think it could work" I said. He put his guitar back in the stand "It is brilliant.

"No question. I just don't know if…" Just then Finley burst into the room.

"Aunt Tina just called. Said she tried both of you but there was no answer. She asked if one of you could call her immediately. It's important," he said. My stomach dropped. Last time I got a call like that my mom was dying. I stood up.

"Thanks Finley," I replied dialing my sister. Tina answered. "What's going on?" I asked.

"Nana was having trouble breathing. She said her heart hurt. Sunrise called an ambulance, and they took her to the ER. I am in the city. Do you think you could go?" she asked.

"On my way," I said.

"On your way where?" Finley asked.

"Nana is in the hospital," I replied.

Gordo looked at his watch. "We have a college call for Luke in half an hour. Should I cancel it," he asked.

"No. You do that. I'll do this," I replied.

"I'm coming," Finley announced.

"I'm not sure that's a good idea" I responded not sure what her state of mind might be.

"What if she doesn't make it? I'm coming." Finley stated putting on his sneakers. We stopped at a nearby bakery. Got her cookies. Arrived thirty minutes later.

The nurse pulled me aside before we entered her room. "She is disoriented. Stress can aggravate early onset dementia. She hit one of the nurses, so we put her on mild sedatives." I nodded processing the situation, trying to figure out how I'd convince Finley to wait outside.

I looked at the nurse's nametag. "Thank you, Lindsey," I responded, "Have they figured out what is wrong with her heart?" I asked.

"Not yet," she responded. "We've run tests. Just waiting for results."

I turned around to talk to Finley, but he'd already gone into her room. I joined him. Her hair was matted. Her face was grey. Her eyes were wild with fear. Finley looked upset and confused. "Honey, I really think you should wait in the hallway," I said.

"No, I am not leaving you," he replied and sat on the window ledge.

"I love you so much. I just really don't think this is a good idea. She wouldn't want you to see her this way," I said shifting my strategy.

"I am staying," he replied resolutely. I approached her bedside,

"Hi Nana, Finley and I wanted to come say hello, see how you are doing? We brought you some cookies," I said.

"I told you to bring my gardening gloves downstairs. Did you do that? Did you?" She pointed at me accusingly, her eyes unfocused and bulging with blame. I looked back at Finley. He looked away from us out the window. His posture stiffened.

"Yes, Nana, I brought them down," I answered.

"Did you really?" she said suspiciously.

"Yes, I did," I replied patiently.

"Good girl," she said. I told her about Finley's cooking class and Luke's lacrosse tournaments. She was mostly quiet. Occasionally blurted out jumbled demands. Twenty minutes later, we said goodbye.

"I love you Great Nana," Finley whispered as we left.

"See you soon," I said. I tried to kiss her cheek, but she pushed me away. Once in the hallway, I apologized, "Finley, I am so sorry. She is on a lot of drugs." He wouldn't look at me.

"It's a hospital. Why don't they help her," he said angrily, "Why don't they *do* something?" I tried to hold his hand. He pulled it away.

"They are trying," I replied. "They gave her medicine to help her calm down,"

"Well, it's obviously not working," he said. His voice was clipped. "So, they just leave her– like that?" he said quivering. Two tear drops hit the linoleum floor.

Lindsey approached us. "I'm so sorry we didn't know earlier but the COVID test we gave your grandmother this morning came back positive. She tested negative when she was admitted."

My mind raced with thoughts. There was no way she would recover. This was it– our final goodbye. She was the only link I had to my mom. She made me crazy, but I did love her. Didn't want her to die. "I'll be right back," I said to Finley. I re-entered the room. Considered putting a mask on. Opted not to.

"Nana, I love you," I said. She seemed far away. "I know," she replied looking past me. Lindsey entered with two orderlies.

"Marge, we need to move you to another unit, okay." Nana tried to sit up,

"Am I going home?" she asked.

"Yes, Nana," I said, "Very soon. I love you." I touched her shoulder not wanting to upset her by getting too close.

"Thank you, Lindsey," I said wiping away my tears. I will come back after I drop my son. I exited the room. Finley and I walked down the hall. He still wouldn't look at me, but he held my hand. Held it down the elevator, through the vestibule and across the parking lot. When we got in the car, he put his head in my lap and cried. She died that night.

Tying Up Loose Ends and Unraveling Old Stories

The next morning, my sister Anna called. "Do you want me to fly up? I know you have your deposition tomorrow," she said.

"No need," I replied, "I called Salvation Army. They will take everything but the mattress. Tina talked to Sunrise, and there's a resident who wants it," I said.

"I don't want this to all fall on you and Tina," Anna said.

"There really isn't a lot. Truly. I'm going there after work this evening to dispose of toiletries and pick up pictures. After that, we are pretty much done," I assured her.

"Thank you," Anna replied. She paused before continuing, "Is it wrong that I feel relieved?" she asked.

"I think we all do. Most of all, Nana. She's wanted the good lord to invite her to dinner. And now he has."

No money. No friends. No service. Yale medical was taking her body. It was a clean exit. That evening, I went to Sunrise one last time. Collected pictures from walls and coffee tables, disposed of adult diapers and said goodbye. She'd survived life more than enjoyed it. Wherever she'd gone was better than here. As I exited, Adam from the front desk stopped me. "I am so sorry for your loss," he said before buzzing me out. His kindness caught me by surprise. Tina and I had addressed the details of her death. Adam was the first to acknowledge our loss.

Loss… the word echoed in my mind as I exited. The sun was setting. I walked to the car. Put knickknacks and pictures on the front seat. Left Sunrise for the last time. Loss was such a small word for the universe it contained. I drove down the highway deep in thought. Out of the dusk, a deer leapt out into my lane. Froze in the headlights. I swerved to miss hitting it. Pictures flew off the passenger seat. Startled, I slowed down. Glanced over to see if anything had broken.

The picture we'd sent Nana from our trip to Venice caught my eye. Finley was six. He had five pigeons eating breadcrumbs off his arms. The photo captured him perfectly– adventurous, impulsive, curious– a pure joy except for the nonstop danger. We'd had to repeatedly tell him to STOP– Stop running across busy streets for gelato. Stop balancing on rickety columns. Stop leaning over the bridge for colored glass. Stop posing on ancient artifacts.

Midway through the vacation, Gordo and I were reading in bed when Luke sat up crying, "Can I talk to you about something," he asked.

"Of course," I said, patting the space in front of me. He came over and sat down.

"I'm afraid if you keep telling Finley to stop being who he is, he's going to become invisible to himself." I stared into Luke's earnest, blue eyes. It was a profound thing to say. Deserved more than some pat parental platitude.

"We just don't want him to get hurt," Gordo explained.

"But we can find other ways to do that," I said, "There is nothing more important than protecting his spirit. AND yours. Thank you, Luke. You are an amazing brother and son." His eyes were still full of worry.

"I just don't want him to disappear," he said, big tears rolling down his cheeks.

I pulled him close, "Me neither. Luke. Me neither."

Life, death, memory, miracles… they lived side by side in every moment. I pulled off at our exit. Got home and emptied the car. I set the pictures on the counter.

Finley put his arm around me when I came in. "Can't imagine how hard today was," he said.

Gordo gave me an extra-long hug. "We ordered you sushi."

"I love you, Mama. Sorry." Luke added.

"Oh my gosh," I suddenly remembered, "How did the college call go? Feels like yesterday was a hundred years ago." I shook my head at the absurdity of how much can happen in a day.

"Good, I guess," Luke replied, "We gave Coach our list of D1 schools. He threw out a couple options. I'm working on my highlight reel tonight." The doorbell rang. Finley answered it.

Luke picked up one of the pictures I'd set on the counter, "Oh my god, I totally remember this trip," he said.

Finley looked over. "I think we all do," he said opening his miso soup. We'd rented a house in Nantucket. Spent five hours in the car and two hours on the ferry. One of the dogs had thrown up and both I-pads had died.

"Didn't we drive up and down the same street– like twenty times?" Luke asked, squeezing soy sauce over his California roll.

"And then you asked some random couple directions, right," Finley added.

"Yup." I replied, "Do you remember what they told us?" I asked.

Luke responded, "That the street we were looking for was a paper road, and we couldn't get there using GPS,"

Gordo passed out chopsticks. "Can't get where you're going using someone else's map," he said smiling at me.

I went to bed early. Woke up Tuesday morning ready for the deposition. I put on mascara and a blue sweater. Set up my computer and clicked join to enter the virtual room. We introduced ourselves. The court reporter swore me in. Opposing counsel started by saying how sorry he was this had happened to Finley and our family. Even over Zoom, his kindness came through. His questions were respectful and compassionate. He doubled back on a few for clarity. I was unshakable in the details. Truth is not hard to remember.

Gordo called me after. "Our attorney said you were flawless. Despite Nora's objections, he had to depose her kids– said they would not come across well at trial. More importantly, the 911 neighbor cried through her deposition. Her son is still terrified of dogs," Gordo said.

"That is terrible– but I guess good for us," I said.

"He thinks we'll have an offer this afternoon," Gordo replied.

I was in a creative briefing when Gordo texted me the news. *We got an offer.* He shared the details. Less than we wanted, more than they wanted– enough to close the case. I gave it the thumbs up. What had begun three years ago would soon be over. I focused back on the briefing.

"Is everyone clear on the strategy?" the account director asked, "The meeting will be next Tuesday." A screen full of faces on mute nodded. I opened my notebook to write down the date and saw Gordo's scribbled note. *IT'S OK. GO WITH IT.* Hard to believe it had been less than a month since that first call with Mack. I wrote down the client meeting date. The account director wrapped up, "Okay then, let's get to work. The client wants big ideas. Big thinking. Big enough to disrupt the category. This is our chance to really shine."

I wanted to shine. Do something big. Bodacious. Purposeful. Not merely churn out more migraine commercials, go to the gym and binge-watch Netflix. Launching a psilocybin empire felt big, but I knew my brilliant plan was nothing more than a pipedream. Plus, what was magic to me about mushrooms had nothing to do with psychedelics. Mushrooms were subversive change-agents. Adaptive. Intuitive. Rooted in benevolent frequencies we couldn't comprehend. They were pioneers healing the natural world through an underground network of mycelium. I wanted to shine like *that.* Instead, I spent the afternoon writing anthemic advertising that heralded the dawn of a headache-free future.

Later that day, I picked up Finley and a couple of his resource friends from school. "How was everyone's day?" I asked.

Bob, who was socially autistic, academically brilliant, and seemingly more adult than me replied, "Some kids will tell you their day was all unicorns and rainbows. I am not one of those kids." I fell immediately in love. Who says that? So matter of fact. So honest.

"Why was it a bad day," I asked.

He didn't miss a beat, "I had a strong reaction to something some kids said and had to spend the afternoon by myself." His face held no affect.

"I'm sorry," I said. "It's okay," he replied, "It happens." I wanted to be that ok with life– with myself. We arrived at the art center. I dropped them off for cartooning.

"Have a good class, guys," I said. They piled out of the car– awkward gaggle of middle-school boys. I watched them walk away– each strange and beautiful– unicorns on their way.